MW00768010

This book is a gift

To: _____

From: _____

Special Occasion

_____

~ The ~
WITNESS CAROL

George DeTellis Jr.
with David Wimbish

This book is a work of fiction. Names, characters, places, and incidents either are products of the author's imagination or are used fictitiously. Any resemblance to actual events or locales or persons, living or dead, is entirely coincidental.

The Witness Carol
copyright © 2016 George DeTellis, Jr. with David Wimbish

ISBN 978-0-9745393-1-7

Editorial development
by Hazard Communications, Inc.,
P.O. Box 568
Round Hill,Virginia, 20142.

Phone: (540)338-7032
Email: Exangelos@aol.com

All rights reserved. No part of this book may be reproduced in any form without permission in writing from the publisher, except in the case of brief quotations embodied in critical articles or reviews.

Printed in the United States of America.

This book is dedicated to my grandparents
Charles and Anna DiPietro.
Your lives have been the greatest witness.

Contents

I. The Discovery 9

II. A Church on Life Support 21

III. The Only Thing Your Church Needs
Is a Decent Burial 29

IV. Oh, No! Not That Guy! .37

V. Lester Gets Enlightened .47

VI. Knock and It Will Be Opened 57

VII. Journey to the Romans Road 63

VIII. Lester and Iris for Jesus 71

IX. Could This Be Revival? .87

X. Let Earth Receive Her King 93

XI. You Are the Light of the World 101

Churches in America 109
Epilogue 111
Reader's Guide 113
The Church Play 117

King David's Prophecy
Psalm 22:30

"A seed shall serve him; it shall be accounted to the Lord for every generation. They shall come and declare his righteousness unto a people that shall be born that he hath done this"

Chapter One

THE DISCOVERY

Thursday, November 15th

It was cold and raining as the mourners slowly spilled out of the church and onto the hilly countryside of central Virginia.

The dull gray of the afternoon sky above the broad Shenandoah Valley, with its patchwork of farms, was a stark contrast to the fiery autumn foliage on the surrounding Blue Ridge Mountains.

Six men in dark suits, shoulders hunched beneath their small load, carried the simple coffin up the hill to the cemetery. Nick Romano was the only one of those men who had not been born and raised within a stone's throw of the small Mennonite Church from which he and the other pall bearers were emerging into the overcast afternoon.

Out in the yard of Singer's Glen Mennonite Church, Nick stepped into a soft spot and his left foot sank in mud up to the top of his shoe. He could feel his muscles strain as he stumbled; then he breathed a silent prayer of thanks as he quickly regained his balance and tightened his grip on the brass handle of the coffin.

Behind them came the mourners. Beyond the low stone wall of the cemetery, a freshly dug gravesite yawned black and moist amidst the rows of plain marble headstones.

Once they'd set the coffin in the straps that would lower it into the grave, Nick's eyes searched the small crowd. There was his wife, Rachel, standing on the oppo-site side of the grave with the women. With her blond hair loosely styled, she stood out among the other women who were all wearing traditional Mennonite head cover-ings. Rachel kept her gaze to the ground, dabbing at her eyes with a cotton handkerchief. Nick wanted to go to her, to stand beside her with his arm protectively around her slender shoulders. But he was careful to respect the traditions and beliefs of his wife's Mennonite roots: tra-ditions and beliefs that kept men gathered on one side of the grave and women on the other. So he stood quietly, his hands clasped behind his back, aware too, that he stood out from the other men with their collarless suits and clean-shaven faces.

Bishop Witmer cleared his throat and began the graveside portion of the funeral. The lengthy service held earlier in the primitive clapboard church had been primarily in German, with a little English interspersed for the benefit of the non-Mennonite visitors.

But it wasn't the differences in culture or language that made Nick feel so alone. Something deeper that had been troubling him for months chose this moment to work its way to the surface.

The nasal drone of the bishop, as he read from *The Minister's Service Book,* drew on one part of Nick's mind while deeper personal matters fought for another place in his thoughts.

"*Servant of God, well done,*" the Bishop read. "*Thy glorious warfare's past…*"

Nick's mind wandered back to their last visit here, when Rachel's grandfather, Isaac Keener, now resting inside this coffin, was still alive and vibrant. Nick had only met him a few times, but he had always admired the old man's fervent spiritual convictions. There was a fire in his old soul that fascinated Nick. Maybe that was why he felt so troubled at this moment.

Rachel had never lost her childlike adoration for her grandfather. She often told stories about watching him at his blacksmith's shop, hammering out horseshoes and plows for the Mennonite community here in Singer's Glen, Virginia.

It was odd, Nick thought, how the man they were about to lower into the ground could be so humble and unassuming yet so firm and alive in his devotion to God.

Nick had never spoken to Isaac without being impressed by the older man's knowledge of the scriptures and his commitment to live out its teachings.

"Grandpa" had lived to be ninety years old. He had raised his children and his grandchildren. But Nick found himself wondering, *What is God's purpose for my life? Is this all there is to it—you raise your family and then die? Isn't there something more than this?*

"*...the battle's fought, the race is won...*" said the Bishop, loudly.

Today, as was true every time he came here, Nick was struck by the differences between his family and Rachel's. Their cultures couldn't have been more different. Rachel's relatives were strong, quiet Mennonites who strove to be gentle and humble in everything they did. He came from a large and boisterous Italian family where nobody minded a little shouting every now and then. Whereas Rachel's family had farmed the Shenandoah Valley between these ridges for nearly 200 years, the Romanos had come to Boston from Italy in the early 1900s.

"*...and thou art crowned at last, Amen.*"

Nick had met Rachel when they were working together as missionaries in Haiti. Nick's father, who was a pastor, had gone to Haiti as a missionary when Nick was still a teenager, and now they'd been there for nearly twenty years. Despite their differences, Nick and Rachel had immediately sensed a mutual attraction—an attraction made stronger by their shared love for God.

But for Nick, something was missing. And it had been missing for some time.

The bishop seemed to be ending the eulogy, and Nick redirected his attention toward the lowering of the coffin. Many of the women were crying openly now, and his heart ached for Rachel in her grief. At her side cousin Greta, her first pregnancy beginning to show, placed a comforting arm around Rachel's shoulders, and Nick was grateful. Every time he and Rachel had visited, these people had proven to be a caring, close-knit community.

As the mourners turned away from the grave to make their way back to the house that Nick thought of as the parsonage, they consoled each other with firm handshakes and quiet embraces. Jacob, Greta's husband, patted Nick on the shoulder as he walked beside him.

"It's a sad day, but a joyous one as well," Jacob said with a grim smile. Nick only nodded, noting that the other man's supply of encouraging proverbs seemed to have dried up. He slowed his step and waited for Rachel.

"Are you all right?" he asked gently. She slipped her hand into his and laid her cheek against his shoulder for a moment.

"Yes, I'll be fine," she answered. "How about you? You okay?"

He kissed the top of her head. "Yes. I'm good," he said and let her pull away to follow the rest of the women into the house. Watching her go, he added to his thought, just a little dead inside, that's all.

At the parsonage, Nick mixed with the men as best he could. But their discussions ranged from farming to plans for a barn raising to the need to cast lots for a new deacon; Nick stood by awkwardly with nothing to contribute.

What could he talk about that these men would connect with? His life as a traveling evangelist? Or that, in spite of the fact that he was out "doing the Lord's work, spreading the Good News", he was really, actually feeling empty and searching inside?

He was ready to leave long before evening when Jacob finally ushered Greta, along with Nick and Rachel, to the horse-drawn carriage in which they'd ridden to the funeral. It would be a long ride back to the farm.

Outside, it had rained. But now the rain had slowed to a light sprinkle as night fell on Singer's Glen. The rhythmic *clip-clop* of the horse's hooves was soothing, and Rachel was soon dozing, resting against Nick's shoulder.

It is good that she is resting, he thought. She had tossed and turned the night before. Their suitcases were already packed, but he would give Rachel a few more moments to visit with Greta and Jacob before leaving for the long drive back to Florida. He figured they could make it to the North Carolina border, three hours south, before stopping for the night.

Jacob halted the carriage in front of the farmhouse, and Nick jumped down to assist Greta and Rachel. After they ascended the wooden steps arm in arm, Nick climbed back into the carriage to ride to the barn with Jacob. He didn't know anything about horses or carriages, but he could at least keep Jacob company and properly thank him for his hospitality.

"I hope Greta will be all right," Nick commented, unable to think of anything else to say.

"Oh, sure. It will be a little tough for a while, what with Isaac being gone. He was always good for lively conversation around the dinner table," Jacob replied, stroking the horse with a grooming brush. "It's a sad day but a joyous one as well."

Nick nodded. "Yes, there's no doubt he's with the Lord. That's a comfort. He was a fine man. Strong convictions. Deep faith."

"There's a truth to what you're saying there, Nick. While most of us seem to have our trials and tribulations that sometimes cause us to waver, Isaac was always steadfast. Never knew him to doubt or to question God. Steady he was. Always the same."

Nick frowned.

He knew what Jacob said was true, but how could it be? How could a man never seem to waver, never falter in his faith? Even King David had his struggles and had written psalms about his hard times. How did Isaac manage to live out his faith so confidently and passionately? What did he know that Nick didn't know?

It was as though Jacob heard Nick's unspoken question.

"From what I've heard my whole life, Isaac had been like that since he was a child. His father, Great-Grandpa Henry Keener, was an evangelist. He went all through Virginia on horseback, stopping in every town and village he came to, just helping out wherever he could. He'd help build fences, shoe horses, pick apples, whatever he could. All the time he was helping people do what they needed to have done, he'd be talking to non-believers about Jesus, urging them toward salvation. And if they were believers, he'd be talking to them about serving and discipleship. On fire for the Lord he was. And Isaac was just like his father."

Nick mulled this over for a moment. Perhaps it was simply that the Scripture was true. *"Raise up a child in the way he should go, and when he is old he will not depart from it."* But still, there had to be more to it than that. Nick had accepted Jesus as his personal savior when he was seven years old and was raised by Christian parents. He hadn't departed from his faith, but he might as well have for all the good he had done lately.

Nick shook his head, his gaze straying around the barn while he listened with one ear to Jacob's endless stream of conversation. The thing that had been troubling him deep down now surfaced in his mind.

Nick, too, was an evangelist. He traveled throughout the United States preaching the gospel and raising money for the family mission in Haiti. As far as he and his family were concerned, telling people about Jesus always had first priority. Fundraising was of secondary importance, even though it was necessary to sustain the work in Haiti.

There had been a time when Nick loved his life of traveling and preaching. But over time he felt his fire reduce to a mere flicker. It was that inner flame he'd felt slowly dying, and now it was threatening to go out completely.

"What happened to my passion?" Nick wondered silently, as he thought about Isaac. What had happened to the sense of zeal and enthusiasm that had driven his adult life for over fifteen years? Now he was tired all the time. His ministry had long ago reached a plateau. It seemed that nothing he did was working to recharge his life or his God-given calling.

Maybe my mission is over, he mused. Maybe I was called to be an evangelist for a time, and that season has passed. Nick shied away from that thought. He knew nothing else. He wanted nothing else.

There in the barn, while Jacob was finishing up with the horses, Nick found himself caught in an inner conflict he didn't want to face.

What was he supposed to do now? He believed he was meant to be an evangelist. But he was burned out—or very close to it. Was there any way to fan what was left of his enthusiasm back into a flame?

Maybe, the thought came, you should just let it go out. Go on to something else in life.

"*Lord, help me,*" he prayed silently. "*Show me the way. Teach me whatever it is I need to learn to do your will.*

Going into all the world to preach the gospel is all I've ever known, all I've ever wanted to do. You know it's never been an option for me. It was my passion. My heart's desire.

"But I'm so tired, Father, and I can't seem to do what I need to do anymore. Please relight the fire inside me. Please use me again. In Jesus' name."

It was a simple prayer, but Nick felt an immediate peace settle over him. He leaned against the wall and gave his attention once more to Jacob, who was still rambling on.

"...so we went ahead and sorted through Isaac's belongings. Lord knows he didn't have much. We saved his Bible to give to Rachel. We thought he would want her to have it. What do you think?"

"Oh," Nick fumbled. "I think she'd be very happy to have Isaac's Bible."

"Good. It's done then," Jacob replied. "And what about you? Is there something of Isaac's you might like?"

"Um, can't think of anything..." Nick was saying.

"I know," Jacob interrupted. "Isaac had many books. Theological works. Inspirational ones, too. I know you like to read, Nick. I'm not much for it, myself. Help yourself to some of Isaac's books. There in a barrel... over there..." He nodded toward a corner of the barn.

If there was one common rule you obeyed in this small community it was this: Never refuse hospitality.

Nick found the barrel in the corner of the barn and lifted off the wooden lid. He had to paw his way down, through a layer of frayed shirts, a broken leather bridle, a pair of eyeglasses with a cracked lens, and other useless items. What books? he wondered.

And just when he was going to quit, his fingers closed around a book. He pulled it out to have a closer look.

It was bound in old leather, a short book, only about a hundred dog-eared and well-worn pages in length. Its black cover was split in several places, and the title had faded so that Nick couldn't read it in the dim light. Opening it, he was surprised to find a hand-written inscription.

"This book is a gift to my children and to my children's children yet to be born. May you discover your power of purpose hidden in God's Word. Psalm 22. Henry Keener." It was dated August 12, 1929.

"Henry Keener?" Nick thought, amazed. Rachel's great-grandfather? How old was this book? If it had been in better condition, it might be worth something. Nick turned to the yellowed title page, which read, *"The Power of Purpose, 1907."* There was no publishing company listed. No copyright. No author. Did Great-Grandpa Henry Keener write this?

Curious, Nick squinted and began reading the first paragraph. As he read, his breath quickened, and his heart felt like it was beating high in his throat.

Could this possibly be? Was this coincidence? Providence?

"Jacob?" he called out, his voice shaking.

"Yeah?"

"I found a book I'd like to have."

A few days later, back home in Florida, Nick was so engrossed in his reading that he didn't hear the quiet knock on his study door.

"Honey?" The door slowly opened and Rachel poked her head into the room.

"Dinner will be ready in five minutes," she said.

"Oh, I'll be right there to set the table."

"Don't worry about it," she laughed. "I've already done it." Her eyes twinkled as she teased him, "That must be some book. You've been hiding in here for hours."

"Have I?" Nick laughed. "Well, you're right. It *is some book.*"

"Five minutes," Rachel said. "Don't forget." She walked out of the room and slowly closed the door behind her.

Reluctantly, Nick shut *The Power of Purpose* and placed it on top of his desk.

For the first time, in a long, long while, he felt something stirring in his spirit. He was almost afraid of letting himself get too excited. He didn't want to be disappointed again.

I've got to go out and see if this works, he thought.

"That's what I'm going to do," he said out loud. "I'm going to get back out there and preach this as if I really do believe it."

And if it doesn't work, he thought, *I'm quitting the ministry and going into real estate.*

Chapter Two

A CHURCH ON
LIFE SUPPORT

Wednesday, December 5th

Pastor Bob McCandlish glanced at his watch as he pulled into the parking lot of Friendship Community Church. It was 7:25 p.m. The midweek prayer service was scheduled to start in five minutes.

And, as usual, there was only one other car in the lot.

That was the battered old yellow Pontiac that belonged to Iris Walker—*Iris's Battleship*, as it was known. She and her late husband had been founding members of this church, and Iris hadn't missed a service in nearly thirty years. Even now, in her mid-seventies, when she didn't like driving after dark, she still managed to make it to church every Wednesday evening. She even had her own key to the church, and she was almost always the first to arrive.

Iris loved the Lord, and she loved her church. She was one vibrant pulse point in a congregation barely hanging on to life—a prayer warrior who would never think about leaving the congregation, no matter what.

Pastor Bob sighed and reached for his well-worn Bible. He had been the pastor here for over twenty-five years. He was feeling his age, and so was the once-impeccable church building. Friendship Community Church was a white A-frame, with an educational wing extending out to the right. It had been a well-known landmark in the city of Santa Cruz ever since its construction more than thirty years ago. But these days, it was badly in need of a facelift. Paint peeled away from the walls. A broken window in one of the classrooms had been covered with cardboard. It was well past the time for the roof to be replaced.

Pastor Bob straightened his tie as he opened the door and walked into the foyer.

Maybe it was just his mood tonight. But, somehow, the carpet seemed more worn and thin than usual. He looked up at the bulletin board, where dozens of faces of people of all ages smiled out at him. These were the faces of missionaries the church supported all over the world. Many of them had grown up in this church. It was here that the Word of God had taken hold in their hearts, and where they had first heard the call to serve the Lord overseas. Yes, this church had once been thriving, full of life. Yet today, they were fortunate to have thirty-five people attend the Sunday morning service.

"Good evening, Pastor."

"Evening, Iris. How are you tonight?"

She sat in her usual place. Third pew, center aisle. "I'm fine. Do you suppose we might be the only two who make it tonight?"

He managed a forced smile. "Well, if that's the case, we'll just pray up a storm, won't we?"

Iris smiled back. "We certainly will."

He didn't doubt for a moment that she really could pray up a storm if she needed to.

Pastor Bob couldn't help but notice how frail she was looking these days. But the fire in her blue eyes showed that her spirit was as strong and vibrant as ever.

He looked around. "It's kind of dark in here, isn't it? Maybe I ought to turn some more lights on."

"They're all on, Pastor."

"They are?"

"Oh, yes. But I'm glad you think it's dark in here, because I was afraid my eyes were getting worse."

The door opened and two couples came in.

"Well, what do you know?" the pastor chimed, in mock surprise. "It looks like we won't be alone tonight after all!"

He was right, they weren't alone. But they didn't have much company either. Eleven people showed up, including Iris and Pastor Bob, and the youngest was a couple in their mid-fifties.

Nobody seemed interested in what was going on; in fact, old Howard Ainsworth slept through the entire service—which reminded Pastor Bob of something he'd once heard somewhere, "Some churches have sound doctrine, but they are sound asleep."

The service was over at 8:30 sharp, and the parking lot was deserted within ten minutes. Nobody hung around to talk. There had been a time when the pastor had to turn the lights off to get people to leave. Even then, they'd retreat to the local coffee shop, or to someone's home, to finish their conversation. These days it was, "Thanks for the lesson, Pastor. See you Sunday," and then the race was on to see who would be the first one out of the parking lot.

The Pastor made a mental note to find out what was on television Wednesday night. He figured he must be missing something good, the way the members of his church all rushed home to watch it.

Getting out of the parking lot was the only time all evening some of those folks showed the least bit of life.

As soon as Pastor Bob had said his farewells to Iris— who was usually the last to leave—he made his way back to his study, a small office to the left of the auditorium.

He sat down at his desk, which was piled high with paperwork, picked up the phone, and began to dial.

Eight…five…nine …

He changed his mind and quickly dropped the phone back into its cradle.

"I've got to do it," he thought. "I promised I'd call him today, and today is almost over."

He let out a long sigh, picked up the phone, and started to dial again.

This time he dialed the first four numbers before he hung up.

RRRING! RRRING!

Pastor Bob was so startled by the ringing of the phone he'd just hung up that he nearly dropped the receiver as he grabbed it.

"Friendship Church. This is Pastor McCandlish. May I help you?"

"Hello, Pastor. It's me."

"Oh, hello, Jim. I…uh…was just going to call you," the Pastor stammered.

"So, did you have a big crowd tonight?" sang the voice on the other end of the line. "What was the paid attendance tonight? Five, six?"

"Eleven."

"Eleven! Wow! How'd you fit 'em all into that auditorium. What does it hold—six hundred?"

"Let's just skip the sarcasm and get down to business," said Pastor Bob.

"I'm only trying to make a point," Jim said.

"Which is?"

"It's about time for you and that board of yours to stop stalling and accept my offer. You just don't need that big building any more."

Pastor didn't respond, so Jim kept talking.

"Two million dollars is a lot of money. You can buy yourself a nice little place somewhere else and start over."

"Yes, I know, but…"

"Oh, by the way, I've got some good news. The city planning commission has just approved my design-plans for the garden apartments I'm going to build on the site."

"We're pretty close to making a decision," the Pastor replied.

"Decision? What decision do you have to make? I don't want to be cruel, but your church has outlived its usefulness. Nobody is interested in hearing your old fashioned ideas about God."

Pastor Bob sighed, "Jim, I know you were raised in the church. I knew your father, and he was a fine man of God."

There was a brief silence before Jim answered.

"I'm sorry if I hurt your feelings, Pastor. But these days, I only believe in what works. And, from where I sit, it's obvious that whatever you're doing over there, it ain't working. You've got my offer. I'll need your answer before the first of the year."

CLICK.

Pastor Bob rolled his eyes toward heaven. For just a moment, his mind flashed back to that happy day when he had walked across the stage at Dallas Theological

Seminary to get his degree. He'd had so much optimism back then. He was going to turn the world upside down for Jesus. And now ...? Well, it wasn't going to do any good to brood about things.

"Help us, Lord," he sighed.

RRRING! RRRING!

The pastor's mouth flew open in surprise. For a moment, he almost expected it to be the Lord on the line. Or, at least, the miracle he'd been praying for.

"Hello?" He answered the phone with a timid waver in his voice.

"Reverend McCandlish?" someone asked.

"Yes?"

"This is Nick Romano."

Romano? That name was familiar. Where had he heard it before?

"I'm calling to follow up on the letter I sent you last week."

Pastor Bob rifled through some papers on his desk. *Ah, yes, here it is. Romano is a missionary who wants to come speak at the church. He's out on a speaking tour, trying to raise money for a mission in Haiti.*

"Yes," the pastor said. "I have it right here."

He felt himself blushing at the thought that he had been naive enough to think this call might be a miracle of some kind—an answer to his prayers.

Miracles, it seemed, were few and far between these days.

Chapter Three

THE ONLY THING YOUR CHURCH NEEDS IS A DECENT BURIAL

"Actually, Pastor," the voice on the other end of the line continued, "I've sent you at least four letters over the past few weeks. And I haven't heard anything, so I decided I'd call you."

Wow! This fellow is certainly persistent.

"I'm sorry, Mr. Romano," the pastor responded. "I'm afraid we're without a church secretary at the moment, and I'm a little bit behind in my correspondence."

The truth was that the previous church secretary had retired six months ago, and there hadn't been enough money to hire another one. Besides, most of his time lately had been taken up dealing with various threatening letters from city officials, demanding that the church take steps to repair a number of building code violations.

"That's okay, Pastor," he heard Romano chuckle. "I understand that you're a busy man. But if you have a moment right now, why don't you check your calendar and let me know when would be a good time for me to come?"

Pastor McCandlish sighed deeply. "I don't want to be rude, but the truth is that this just isn't a good time. Especially not with Christmas just around the corner."

"But actually, I've found that..."

"I'm sorry," the pastor interrupted. "To be completely honest with you, we're not doing very well financially right now. Attendance is down, and there is no way we could pay your travel expenses or provide an honorarium."

There was no reaction on the other end of the phone, so the pastor kept on talking.

"The bottom line is, if you're looking to raise money for your work in Haiti, I'm afraid you'd be wasting your time by coming here.

"Listen, Pastor," Nick responded, "something happened to me recently...and for the first time in a long while, I'm really excited about reaching people for Christ. I think I could get the members of your congregation excited, too, if you'd just let me come and preach."

Now it was the pastor's turn to laugh. "I appreciate your enthusiasm," he said, "but, like I said, we couldn't even pay your travel expenses."

"That's all right," Romano said. "A friend of mine works for United Airlines, and she gave me a 'friends and family pass', so I can travel for free during the next six months."

"United Airlines doesn't fly into Santa Cruz," Pastor McCandlish replied. "In fact, nobody flies into Santa Cruz because we don't have an airport."

"I'll take the Super Shuttle from San Francisco International."

"Well, I really don't know if..."

"How about Sunday after next?"

Pastor McCandlish chuckled again. "It seems to me that you're determined to come no matter what I say."

"Pretty much."

"Okay, Mr. Romano. I'll put you on the calendar. I could use a Sunday off, anyway."

"Great!"

"One thing, though," the pastor cautioned.

"Yes?"

"Don't expect too much from this congregation. I wouldn't want you to lose your new found excitement."

Thursday morning. The heavy coastal fog was just beginning to burn off when the pastor pulled his ten-year-old white Mercury Sable into the parking lot at Denny's restaurant.

It was the kind of morning that made the ache in his soul grow deeper. It was on mornings like this that he and his wife, Rita, used to put off the worries of the world for a while and go for long strolls along the beach, hand in hand. Sometimes, younger couples would smile at them and give each other a nudge, as if to say, "Aren't they cute?"

He guessed it was strange to see an older couple strolling barefoot in the sand, holding hands as if they were young sweethearts. But neither one of them cared that much what others thought, even when some members of the church suggested that such behavior was too "undignified" for a pastor.

Life had never been the same—not even close— since Rita's death from breast cancer four years ago. How he wished he could go strolling on the beach with her this morning. But instead, he was here at Denny's getting ready to meet with Roy Smythe, the head of the church's board of elders.

Smythe was early, as always. The distinguished-looking, gray-haired gentleman was already seated inside. He glanced out the window and nodded when he saw Pastor McCandlish getting out of his car. Smythe was retired now after a long and successful career as a corporate executive for Sunbeam. You didn't have to look at him twice to know he was a success. And his success extended to everything he did, including his role in the church. He was tall, imposing, very articulate, and had a deep, booming voice that commanded respect.

Roy had winced when Pastor Bob recommended they meet at Denny's. He was accustomed to finer places. Finally, he'd smiled and said, "Sure, why not."

He raised his coffee cup in something of a salute as Pastor McCandlish approached his booth.

"Top of the morning to you."

"Morning, Roy. How are things with you?"

"Personally? Couldn't be better." He took a long sip of coffee. "I only wish the church was doing as well."

"Me, too," the pastor replied, as the waitress came with Roy's breakfast.

"You don't mind that I went ahead and ordered, do you?" Roy asked.

Pastor Bob smiled politely. "Of course not. Go right ahead and eat."

"Are you ready to order, sir?" asked the waitress.

"I'll need a few more minutes," the pastor said. "But I will have a cup of coffee, please."

"Certainly."

Roy dug into his meal without even pretending to say grace. Even though Pastor Bob didn't judge people on whether or not they prayed before meals, he did think about how typical of Roy that was. In all the years he'd known Roy, he'd never seen him make a public confession of his faith. In fact, he wasn't really certain that Roy had ever surrendered his life to Christ. Roy was self-confident, assured. Always knew where he was headed and how to get there. It was difficult to imagine that he had ever reached a point where he realized his need for Christ.

Every time they talked about what it meant to be a Christian, Roy danced all around the subject. He knew what to say, but his words seemed to lack something; maybe it was conviction. Roy and his wife, Rosemary, had started attending "Friendship Church" ten years ago when they had just moved to Santa Cruz and needed friends. But it had never been clear if his involvement in the church went further than that.

As a good businessman, Roy had helped guide the congregation through a number of tight financial situations over the past few years, and Pastor Bob was grateful for that. At the same time, he wished that Roy would show as much concern about the spiritual health of the church as he did about its financial health.

"So, did you talk to Jim last night?" Roy asked, between bites of his pancakes.

"Yes. I told him we needed some more time to think about things."

Roy nodded. "Last time I spoke with him, I told him we needed some time to find another building to rent. And you know what he said? He said, 'Roy, the only thing your church needs is a decent burial.'"

Roy took another bite of his pancakes.

"And what hurts me the most," he said, "is that I'm afraid he's probably right."

The waitress was back.

"Have you made up your mind, sir?"

"I think I'm just going to stick with the coffee. I really don't have much of an appetite this morning."

The waitress shrugged. "If you change your mind, let me know."

"Thanks. I will."

Roy had already cleaned his plate. For someone who was hurting, Pastor Bob thought, he certainly didn't show it.

"You know," Roy said, dabbing at his mouth with his napkin, "the church had to borrow money again to pay our bills last month."

Then he reached into his pocket and fished out an official looking envelope.

"And here's the latest threatening letter from the city. Picked it up at the post office this morning. Now they're saying that if we don't get everything up to code within sixty days, they're going to condemn the church property."

"Sixty days?" the pastor sputtered. "Let me see that list."

He knew what was on it, of course. He'd seen it all before. And he knew that it was going to cost a whale of a lot of money to fix things—especially the roof problem: it alone would cost over $200,000. There was no way the remaining members of Friendship Church could ever raise that kind of money.

"I've sounded out some of the members to see how they feel," Roy said. "Most of them seem to think it would be a good idea to sell and try to rent a building somewhere else. In fact, a lot of the folks I've talked to think that a new location might help us gain some new members."

The pastor sighed, "I don't know. I'd hate to do it, but sometimes I think we should sell the church property for

$2 million, give the money to the Missions Board, and close the doors forever. That way, at least we'd know the money was going for something important."

They sat in silence for a moment, before Pastor Bob remembered the strange phone call he'd received from evangelist Nick Romano the night before.

"I hope you told him not to come," Roy said.

The pastor laughed. "I tried to, but he wouldn't listen."

Roy shook his head. "Well, I wonder how he's going to feel after he comes here?"

"Probably just like we feel," said Pastor Bob. "disappointed."

Chapter Four

OH, NO!
NOT THAT GUY!

Saturday, December 15th

It was a little past nine in the evening when Nick's Super Shuttle finally pulled up in front of the Santa Cruz Days Inn.

As Nick stood waiting for the driver to unload his suitcase, his stomach growled loudly, reminding him that he hadn't eaten since breakfast.

As he counted out his fare and the driver's tip, Nick asked, "Is there any place around here to get a decent meal?"

The driver, a tall, dark, thin man with a handlebar mustache, paused a moment and scratched the back of his head.

Then his face brightened and he pointed.

"Waffa How," he said. They were the first two words he'd said since they left the airport, and Nick didn't understand them. The man had a very thick accent, but Nick wasn't really sure what it was. Armenian, perhaps? Iranian? Indian? Pakistani?

His nametag didn't make it any clearer. "Fawad," it read. What kind of name was that?

Nick turned to see what Fawad was pointing at, and there were the old familiar yellow letters, "Waffle House." That would do just fine.

Fawad thanked Nick for the tip, got back in the van, and drove off.

It was after 10:00 p.m. by the time he had checked in to his room and then made the short walk to the Waffle House, where he took a seat at the counter. The place was deserted except for the thirty-something-year-old standing behind the counter with a spatula in his hand.

Nick chuckled when he glanced at the clock on the wall and saw the sign beneath it: "Nobody will ever steal this clock—because the help are always watching it."

The guy behind the counter seemed to be the cook, the cashier, and the waiter. He wore faded jeans and a lumberjack-style plaid shirt. A dirty white apron was tied loosely around his waist, and long, straight, blond hair spilled out of his chef's cap, which seemed a couple of sizes too small.

He had an open, friendly face and a warm smile. "Evenin.'"

"Good evening," Nick replied. "Not so busy tonight, huh?"

"No sir," the cook replied. "We ain't busy a' tall. Why we was busy about seven o'clock when a bunch of Christmas shoppers come in, and then another bunch come in around eight o'clock. Or maybe it was seven forty-five. Anyways, it don't matter to me, because when we ain't busy I got time to think. And I like taking time to think, don't you?"

"Well I…"

"I used to be night clerk over at the Days Inn, and I loved that job because it gave me lots and lots of time to think. Except sometimes it would get real busy. You know what I mean? Hey, you're new around these parts, ain't you? I ain't never seen you before. Well, my name is Lester."

He held out his hand and Nick took it.

"I'm Nick Romano," he said. But what he was really thinking was, "Have I bumped into a close relative of Gomer Pyle—or maybe Forrest Gump?"

"Romano?" Lester asked. "I used to know a guy named Tony Romano. Is he your cousin?"

"Well, I don't think so…"

"He was a real nice guy."

"I'm sure he was," Nick nodded. "Uh, listen, do you think I could order a grilled chicken sandwich?"

"Well sure! Order anything you want. A grilled chicken sandwich. A cheeseburger. A ham and cheese on rye. Hey, you want a waffle? We specialize in waffles. That's why we're called the Waffle House. We got regular waffles, Belgian waffles, blueberry waffles, pecan waffles…"

Fortunately, Lester's monologue was cut short when a couple came in the front door.

"Howdy, Mr. and Mrs. Johnston," Lester sang out. Apparently, they were regulars. "How y'all doing?"

"We're fine, Lester," the woman smiled. "How's your mother?"

"Oh she's fine. Just fine. 'Cept, you know, she worries about me when I have to work late. Oh, my, where are my manners? This is my new friend, Nick."

Mr. Johnston nodded a greeting in Nick's direction. The smirk on his face seemed to say, *So you've met Lester have you? Had a chance to order yet?*

Lester turned back to Nick. "Now what was that you wanted? A grilled chicken sandwich?"

"That's it." Nick was astounded that Lester got it right.

Lester poured the Johnston's their coffee and then turned around to face the grill, fumbling with the fixings of Nick's sandwich, but that didn't keep him from talking, or even slow him down.

Nick discovered that Lester was thirty-four, and still lived at home with his mother. He'd never known his father, who took off for parts unknown a couple of weeks before Lester was born.

It was obvious from the Johnstons' reactions to Lester that he was Santa Cruz's version of Huckleberry Finn. He had grown up on the wrong side of town and had always been a bit of an outcast, looked down on by the "proper" citizens.

They were nice to him, but in a condescending sort of way. If it bothered Lester, he didn't let on. He seemed to be used to it.

Nick looked at his watch. Now it *was* getting late. He quickly ate his sandwich and then made his way to the cash register to pay his bill.

As Lester keyed in the total, he said, "Hey, Mr. Nick, you never did tell me what brung you to Santa Cruz?"

"Oh, well, as a matter of fact I'm speaking tomorrow at Friendship Community Church. The service starts at 10 o'clock. I'd love to see you there."

Lester shrugged as he handed Nick his change. "Gee, I don't know. I don't get off work until 7:00 a.m."

Nick smiled. "Lester, God has a special purpose for your life. If there's any way you can be there to hear me preach, please come."

Lester's eyes grew wide. He didn't say anything, but it was easy to see what he was thinking. "*God? A special purpose for my life?*"

"Thanks for the sandwich, and the conversation" Nick said. He nodded at Mr. and Mrs. Johnston, still lingering over their coffee, and walked out into the night.

9:00 a.m. Sunday, December 16th

When Nick found out from the Days Inn desk clerk that the church was within a mile of his hotel, he declined Pastor Bob's offer to pick him up on Sunday morning.

The weather was crisp and pleasant, and Nick figured the walk would help to clear the jet-lag cobwebs that seemed to be wrapped around his brain.

But when he arrived at Friendship Community Church—ten minutes before the service was supposed to start—he was surprised that the parking lot was completely empty.

Even so, the door was open, so he went on inside, made his way into the auditorium, and sat down on the front row.

Several minutes ticked by, and only a few people arrived.

Nick frowned and glanced at his watch again. Had he misunderstood? Maybe the service was supposed to start at 10:30? He looked around at the large auditorium, which was sprinkled with a handful of people. Eight or nine of them at most.

The back door swung open, and a distinguished-looking elderly gentleman walked in. He looked around, spotted Nick, and strode up with his hand out. "Mr. Romano?" he asked.

"That's right," Nick said, as they shook hands.

"I'm Bob McCandlish."

"Glad to meet you, Pastor. I was wondering if I had made a mistake."

"No mistake," the pastor assured him. "It just looks like everybody's running a little late this morning. Why don't you come on back to my office for a few minutes, and we can discuss the order of the service?"

When they were seated in the pastor's office, Reverend McCandlish said, "I want to apologize for getting off to a late start this morning. You see, our pianist, Mrs. Edwards, depends on her nephew to swing by and drive her to church, and he's almost always running late. Obviously, we can't start the service until she gets here."

"I understand, Pastor. I'll just go with the flow."

The two men discussed the order of worship for a few moments, and then Pastor McCandlish sighed and said, "You told me over the phone that you have a message that will get this church excited. I certainly hope you're right about that. This congregation has seen better days. Much, much better days."

"What happened?"

"I don't know, really." The pastor shook his head. "Most of the young people have drifted away. The ones who are still here have lost their enthusiasm."

"But I've heard great things about this church," Nick said. "My father told me…"

"Oh, this church has a tremendous history," the pastor interrupted. "We've sent missionaries all over the world and still find a way to support most of them. But people just aren't committed the way they used to be."

He sighed, leaned back in his chair, and stared at the ceiling for a moment, before continuing.

"We'll be lucky if we have fifty people here this morning," he said. "I can't remember the last time the offering brought in enough to pay our bills for the week.

In fact, we may have to shut the doors forever. But why am I telling you all this?"

"Well, I appreciate your honesty," Nick began. Before he could say anything further, the strains of "*Blessed Assurance*" drifted in from the sanctuary. It was 10:20. The pianist had arrived.

Pastor Bob stood up, straightened his tie, and said, "Follow me."

He led Nick out the door and up onto the podium, motioning for him to be seated in a chair just to the right of the pulpit. As Nick looked out over the congregation, he couldn't help but count—and that made him realize just how well Pastor Bob knew his flock. He had said they would be lucky to have fifty in attendance. There were forty-nine people scattered throughout a sanctuary built to hold at least ten times that many.

When the music faded, Pastor Bob stepped to the pulpit.

"Good morning," he said in his cheeriest voice.

"Good morning," the congregation mumbled in reply.

"Today," the pastor continued, "we're fortunate to have a guest speaker who has come a long way…"

As the pastor continued his introduction, the back door to the church swung open with a bang and a latecomer made his way into the sanctuary.

"Well, what do you know?" Nick thought. "Pastor Bob hit it right on the button. Fifty people, just like he said."

Suddenly, a quiet murmur arose from the "assembled congregation."

It was Lester. The cook from the Waffle House. The village ne'er-do-well.

He shuffled down the aisle and took a seat on the next-to-last pew.

All eyes were upon him.

And it was immediately apparent to Nick that most of the people in the pews did not want him there.

As far as he could tell, there was only one person in the entire congregation with a welcoming smile on her face. That, of course, was Iris Walker.

Chapter Five

LESTER GETS ENLIGHTENED

Sunday, December 16th

It took five minutes for the coughing and fidgeting to subside.

Pastor McCandlish continued his introduction, but most of those present weren't paying the slightest attention. Their eyes were focused on Lester. He was about as welcome as a wolf at a sheep's convention, but if he noticed, he didn't let on.

He winked at Nick and smiled. As Nick looked around the sanctuary again, he saw the one other smiling face. An older woman who was also smiling at Nick. He'd met her before church this morning, what was her name? Oh, yes. Iris. She was holding a pen and a small notebook.

Her Bible rested on the pew beside her. Everything about her said, *I want to know more of God's Word. I'm ready to listen and learn.*

Everyone else was still staring at Lester, whispering things like, *Who is that?* and *What is he doing here?*

"Ahem!" Nick cleared his throat in a bid to regain their attention.

"I want to ask you a question this morning," Nick began. "What is God's purpose for your life?"

One or two faces took on a thoughtful look.

"Let me ask you a second question," he said. "Is your life a random act or do you have a destiny?"

The whispering stopped and the sanctuary grew quiet. As Nick paused, it seemed as if more and more members of the church pondered his simple but important questions.

"Before we consider these questions too deeply," Nick continued, "I want to tell you a little bit about who I am, and why I'm here."

He stepped out from behind the pulpit.

"As your pastor told you, my name is Nick Romano. My family is from Boston, although I now live in Florida. My father's father came to America from Italy after the turn of the century. He was barely out of his teens and didn't speak a word of English."

Now every eye was riveted on him. Some had that where-is-he-going-with-this? look. But for the moment, most everyone seemed interested.

"My grandfather had no formal education. He never owned a home. He never knew how to drive a car. But he managed to care for his wife and six children by selling ice and kerosene from door to door. When my father was sixteen years old, a car crashed into my grandfather's old ice wagon and killed him instantly.

"After that, my grandmother and her children wound up living in the projects of South Boston. They were terribly poor, physically and spiritually. You see, my grandfather didn't believe in God and had not set foot in a church since coming to America. The Romano family was completely without hope.

"But, one Saturday afternoon, not too long after my grandfather was killed, three women came and knocked on my grandmother's door. They were Christians who told my grandmother about Jesus. Those women invited my grandmother to come to church. That's what she did, and there she gave her heart to Jesus.

"Every Sunday after that, she was in church, with her six children sitting beside her. My grandmother was never the same after that day.

"I remember once, when she was in her eighties, she asked one of my sister's boyfriends if he was a Christian. 'Grandma,' he said, 'I'm an agnostic. I don't know that there is a God.' She pointed to her chest and, with her thick, Italian accent, she replied, 'I know there is a God. I'ma sure, because He lives insida my heart.'"

There were smiles and nods, and a few warm chuckles. They were with him now.

"Well, it wasn't long before my father surrendered his heart to Christ—and felt God calling him into the ministry.

"My father served as a pastor in Massachusetts for more than twenty-five years. In that time, hundreds of people came to know the love of Christ through his ministry. But when I was eighteen years old, my dad felt that God was calling him to Haiti to be a missionary. Haiti? Where was that? I had to look it up. I was shocked.

"Haiti is the poorest nation in the Western Hemisphere. A place where people are hungry. Where they don't have things like running water, electricity and plumbing. Haiti is a land of Voodoo and repression. I didn't want to go to Haiti!"

He stopped and took a sip from the glass of water that had been placed on the pulpit for him. Then he went on: "But, apparently, it *was* what God wanted. My family has been living and working there for twenty years now. The Lord has used us to build schools, to feed the hungry, and, most importantly of all, to bring thousands of hearts out of the darkness and into the light of God's love.

"I know, and my family knows, that none of this would have happened without those three women who knocked on my grandmother's door in that project in South Boston. Because those women had the courage to knock on someone's door, thousands of people have come to accept Christ as Savior and will live with Him forever!"

KNOCK! KNOCK! KNOCK!

Nick knocked hard on the pulpit three times.

"Their simple knock on that door in South Boston is still echoing into all eternity! I don't know those women's names, but when I get to heaven, I will meet them face-to-face, and I'll enjoy telling them that I'm part of their inheritance. That I wouldn't be there if it wasn't for their faith and courage."

He paused and waited for that thought to sink in.

AH-AH-AH-AH-CHOOOOO!

Lester's loud sneeze shattered the quiet and caused about a half-dozen people to leap off their pews in fright.

Nick had been building to a point, and though the sneeze didn't bother him, it did break his preaching pace. Off-handedly, as a courtesy more than anything, he said, "God bless you, brother ... "

Unknown to Nick, something happened in that brief moment—something miraculous inside Lester. He had been listening to Nick's sermon, but when someone as important in Lester's eyes as a respectable man in a pulpit stopped to notice him and say, "God bless you", it was as if a door long closed in Lester's heart began to open.

Nick Romano, who had no way of knowing that his words were cutting deep, continued to speak. He didn't realize how much Lester understood what it was like to grow up without a father. That he knew what it meant to do without things that other people took for granted. Or that he had always longed to know that someone—besides his mother—cared about him and loved him. He had never even considered that God loved him.

"Now let's get back to the two questions I asked," Nick said. "Is your life a random act or do you have a destiny? And if you do have a destiny, what is God's purpose for your life?

"The answer is that God has a plan for each and every one of us. He says so in the twenty-ninth chapter of Jeremiah: For I know the plans I have for you—plans to prosper you and not to harm you—plans to give you hope and a future."

Nick swallowed hard, hoping he was getting through to his audience, and went on: "But the fact is…if you have never surrendered your life to Jesus Christ, your life is like a feather bouncing around in the winds of chance. It is only when you surrender yourself to Christ that you are baptized, christened if you will, into your eternal destiny! This is so important: God has a plan for every Christian—a plan that, if carried out, will reverberate for good through all eternity!"

He paused and looked out over the congregation. He wanted so badly for everyone to understand what he was saying. But, from what he could tell, it didn't seem to be happening. A few of them seemed to be deep in thought; it was true. But some were thumbing through their hymnals. And one or two were making fold-up toys out of their Sunday church bulletins.

Well, he couldn't stop now!

"A few months ago," he said, "I had reached the point where I was just lurching along through life, doing the best I could, and hoping that God would bless me. Then I made a discovery that changed everything."

He held up a tattered copy of an old book.

The title was barely discernible: *The Power of Purpose.*

"This book is over ninety years old," Nick said. "And it contains wisdom that our generation has largely forgotten. It referred me back to the twenty-second Psalm, where I rediscovered God's plan for my life. The first verse of this Psalm refers to Christ's atoning death on the cross."

He opened his Bible and read, "'My God, my God, why hast Thou forsaken me?' Those are some of the last words that Jesus spoke on the cross," he said. "Then, in the seventeenth verse, we read, 'I may tell all my bones: they look and stare upon me. They part my garments among them, and cast lots upon my vesture.' This is clearly a prophecy of events that occurred when our Lord was crucified. And if we continue reading, we find these comforting words in verse twenty-seven: 'All the ends of the world shall remember and turn unto the Lord: and all the kindreds of all the nations shall worship before thee.'"

He paused so the one or two people who were reading along with him would have time to scan the passage. He was surprised to see that Lester had taken a

Bible out of the rack in front of him. It had taken quite a bit of page turning for him to find the book of Psalms, but he'd done it, and now his lips were moving as he silently read along.

"But what I really want you to notice," Nick continued, "is what it says in the thirtieth verse, 'A seed shall serve him; it shall be accounted to the Lord for every generation. They shall come and declare his righteousness unto a people that shall be born, that he hath done this.'"

Nick held his Bible up with his left hand.

"We who belong to Christ are that seed," he said. "Our destiny is to declare what God has done! We are to declare the Good News of Christ's atoning death to those who were not yet born when He died for them—in other words, to our generation! The knock at the door of my grandmother's house is still echoing today. I don't know who those women were. I don't know their names. But they fulfilled this prophecy in my life. When I get to heaven, I'll meet them face-to-face, and we'll rejoice together that thousands of people have eternal life because of that one day of obedience."

He pointed at the congregation. "Once you give your life to Christ, you have an eternal destiny, and the life you live will affect eternity," he said. "So many of us feel inadequate. 'I don't have a Bible degree.' 'I'm not ordained.' 'I'm too old.' 'I'm too young.' 'I'm too poor.' Our consciousness of our own unworthiness cripples us from reaching out and telling somebody about Jesus. Whoever you are—a student, a businessman, a cook—you have a sphere of influence that God has given only you. No one can impact the people in that sphere the way you can."

He put the Bible down and picked up his copy of *The Power of Purpose.* "This book awakened me to my divine destiny," he said. "It helped me understand that far too many of us are missing out on what God wants us to accomplish. We are doing everything we can to tell people in foreign lands about the salvation that comes only through faith in Christ—and that's good—but we are neglecting our own neighborhoods. It is like we are sending food to Africa, to Asia, and to South America, but the people we come in contact with every day— our friends and neighbors—are starving! Evangelism is nothing more than one beggar telling another beggar where to find food. I've brought enough copies of this book for all of you. I hope you'll all read it. If you put it into practice, I know it will revolutionize your life—and it will bring new life to this church!"

He paused, "This morning, I'm knocking at your door, and I'm giving you an invitation to give your life to Jesus Christ, to enter into your eternal destiny. Will you…"

He never finished the sentence.

Lester stood up.

"Yes!" he shouted. "Yes! I'll give my life to Jesus!"

Chapter Six

KNOCK AND IT WILL BE OPENED

Lester wept openly, without embarrassment or shame, as Nick led him through the prayer of salvation.

"This is the happiest day of my life," he blubbered. "I'm so glad you wanted that grilled-chicken sandwich last night."

Nick hugged him, and then, together, they made their way to the foyer of the church.

Pastor Bob came to the podium to make a few announcements and then dismissed the congregation with a blessing. "I want to thank Reverend Romano for this fine sermon," he began.

Back in the foyer, Nick whispered to Lester. "Just stand here next to me so everyone will have a chance to meet you. And if you don't mind, you can help me pass out copies of the book." He gestured to a large stack of photocopies of *The Power of Purpose.*

Lester, still rubbing tears from his eyes, nodded. "Sure, I'll do anything," he said.

"Remember, a week from this Monday is our Christmas Eve service," said Pastor Bob. "Now, may God's peace be with you. You are dismissed."

Iris Walker was the first one to the back of the church. She threw her arms around Lester's neck and kissed him on the cheek.

"I'm so happy for you!" she said. "Welcome to the family."

Then she turned to Nick. "Thank you so much for that message. It really spoke to me."

Nick handed her a copy of *The Power of Purpose.*

"I can't wait to read this," she said

Pastor McCandlish was also enthusiastic.

He gave Lester a warm hug. "You made a decision today you'll never regret," he said. Then, turning to Nick, "That was a sermon we all needed to hear—including me."

Unfortunately, most of the members of the congregation didn't seem to share his enthusiasm.

As they filed through the foyer on their way out the door, most of them gave Lester a half-hearted handshake and mumbled a few words in Nick's direction.

"Thanks for the sermon."

"Good lesson, Rev'rend."

"Nice having you with us today."

As Lester helped him hand out the photocopies, Nick was discouraged to see that most of the church members didn't seem to know what to do with them. A few stuck them down in their Bibles—where Nick figured they'd find them again next Sunday and wonder where they'd gotten them.

Some of the men almost seemed nervous, as if he were handing them a bill to pay.

"Oh, well," Nick thought. "All I can do is plant the seed."

Half an hour later, Nick was seated at a booth in a nearby Olive Garden Restaurant. Pastor Bob and Iris Walker sat across from him.

Pastor Bob, who seemed to be deep in thought, nibbled on a breadstick while Iris chatted about Nick's sermon. Iris's overflowing enthusiasm was, in fact, the reason the pastor had asked her to join them for lunch.

"I can't even begin to tell you how thrilled I was to hear what you had to say this morning, Reverend Romano," she said.

"Please just call me Nick," he protested.

"You know, our church hasn't been doing very well over the last few years, and…" Iris began.

"No, it sure hasn't." Before she could finish her thought, Pastor Bob chimed in with his agreement.

He suddenly pointed the un-nibbled end of his breadstick at Nick. "I believe God brought you here for a purpose," he said.

"So do I!" Iris agreed. "So do I!"

Pastor Bob took another bite of his breadstick.

"But do you really think this message will work in this day and age?" he asked.

Nick sighed. "Well, to tell you the truth, Pastor McCandlish, I've never done this before. I just found this old book a few weeks ago, and it was so exciting. It made me think that if I could just find a church that would try this message."

"You were right," Pastor Bob interrupted. "You had to come to our church this morning. But now you have to deliver the results."

Nick was startled. "Deliver the results? What do you mean?"

"Look," said Pastor Bob. "We need help. I want you to stay around, just for a week or so, and help us put this message into practice."

Nick reached into his suit pocket, pulled out his daily planner and flipped it open to stall for time. Before he even looked, Nick knew he didn't have another speaking engagement for three weeks.

"You can stay in my guest room," Iris gushed, "and I'll fix all your meals."

Even though Nick was eager to get back home to his wife and children, he was intrigued by the possibilities.

Could this church *really* be brought back to life? Maybe this was the opportunity he was looking for to put Great-Grandpa Keener's *Power of Purpose* to the test.

"I'm a very good cook, Rev.…er…Nick," Iris continued. "What do you say?"

"Well, I have to tell you I'm tempted by the cooking," Nick laughed. "Okay," he said, "you've talked me into it, as long as it's okay with my wife."

Iris raised her glass of iced tea in a salute. "Hooray!" she said. "When can we start?"

The rest of that day and the next, Nick, Pastor Bob, and Iris made as many calls as possible, inviting members of the congregation to an important meeting on Tuesday night at seven. Many of the people they called had gotten to the point where they only attended church on Easter and Christmas, and sometimes not even then. Even so, they were still on the church's membership roll.

Most of the people made excuses why they couldn't come to the meeting, but a few said that they might be able to, perhaps, maybe, if every little thing in their lives went perfect that day.

Chapter Seven

JOURNEY TO THE ROMANS ROAD

Tuesday, December 18th

When Tuesday evening rolled around, Iris and Nick rode to the church together in her "battleship."

The entire four miles of the trip, Nick had to fight the tendency to ask if he could please take over the wheel. She drove *so slowly!* At one point, they hit her top speed of forty-eight miles per hour, but when Iris noticed, she quickly slowed back down to thirty-five.

She glanced over at Nick and smiled. "I don't like to drive too fast," she said.

That was an understatement. But then again, so was her promise that she was "a very good cook." She was way beyond "very good."

As Iris pulled her yellow Pontiac into the parking lot, her headlights revealed a man standing on the sidewalk in front of the building, waiting to be let in.

The figure waved at them as they got out of the car.

"Hey, Nick! Hey, Iris!"

"Lester," Nick said. "How ya doin'?"

"Never been better!" he said. "My boss gave me the evenin' off so I could come to the meetin'."

"That's great!" Nick said. He grabbed Lester and gave him a playful bear hug, as Iris walked over and unlocked the church door.

"I read it!" Lester said. "I'm a slow reader, but I read every word. Now I wanna get out there and start tellin' people 'bout Jesus."

Nick patted him on the back. "I have a feeling God is really going to use you, Lester."

Lester's face broke into a huge grin. "Really?" he said. "God use me?"

Iris opened the church door wide and motioned for the men to come on inside.

"Oh, Lester," she said, "I almost forget. I have something for you. It's in the car. Let me go get it."

"You got somethin' for me?" Iris hurried to her car and returned with a brand-new, leather-bound Bible.

"Wow, it's beautiful!" Lester said. "Look, it's got red letters and gold on the pages."

At ten minutes past seven, Pastor Bob stood up and said, "Obviously, we were all hoping for a much better turnout. But it looks like it's just going to be the four of us. I guess we might as well get started."

He led the small group in an earnest opening prayer, asking God's blessing on their endeavor. Then, he said, "Nick, I'm just going to turn things over to you."

Nick was disappointed, too, but he tried his best not to let it show.

"We have to trust that God has brought the people He wants to be here tonight," he began. "And we also have to know that if He used the twelve apostles to turn the entire world upside down, he can use the four of us to transform the city of Santa Cruz, California."

He opened his Bible. "I want to start off by reading from the sixth chapter of Mark: 'And he called unto him the twelve, and began to send them forth two by two…'" He gently closed his Bible. "As we see here, when Jesus commissioned the twelve apostles, He sent them out in pairs. I believe that's an important principle. Tonight, God is commissioning us to go out, two by two, to take the good news of salvation through Christ to our friends and neighbors here in Santa Cruz."

Iris smiled at Lester, who was sitting beside her, and said, "We'll make a great team!"

"We sure will!" Lester agreed.

"As you know," Nick continued, "*The Power of Purpose* is all about taking the gospel from house to house, knocking on doors and telling people about Jesus. When you do this, you are unlocking the power of the prophecy found in Psalm twenty-two. As we knock on the physical doors of people's homes, we can count on the Holy Spirit to knock on the spiritual doors of their hearts.

"The Bible has much to say about what you are about to do. 'How beautiful are the feet of them that bring good news.' 'Knock and it shall be opened unto you.' 'And you shall be my witnesses in Jerusalem, Judea, and the whole world.'"

He smiled, "There is no limit to what you can do for God's Kingdom. All God asks of you is an open heart and a willingness to let Him work through you. And remember, too, that you have the good news that everyone needs to hear. Some people may laugh at you or make fun of you. They may just turn their backs on you and leave you standing there. But most people will listen if they know you're sincere, and, as they listen to you, they'll hear God's Holy Spirit talking to them, and the truth will take hold in their hearts."

Lester raised his hand.

"Yes, Lester?"

"I don't mind going out and knocking on doors. But what do I say if someone invites us in? I mean, this is all new to me, and I sure don't want to mess things up. My mama has always said to me, 'Lester,' she'll say, 'the best way to make people think you're smart is to keep your mouth shut.' In other words, if you don't know anything about something, but go ahead and pretend like you do, people are going to see right through that, and they'll…"

"I understand," Nick cut him off. "I was just going to get to that."

Nick handed each of them a fresh copy of *The Power of Purpose*. "Here is the Romans Road to Salvation that I discovered in *The Power of Purpose*," he said. "This ancient method of leading people to Christ is based entirely on the Book of Romans. It all begins with the tenth verse of the third chapter. I suggest that you mark that verse in your Bible, and then mark the next verse you'll need, and so on…"

Lester took out his brand-new Bible, and, with a little help from Iris, quickly found the Book of Romans.

When everyone had turned to Romans 3:10, Nick read,

"'As it is written, There is none righteous, no, not one.'"

He looked up and said, "Now let's go to the twenty-third verse of the same chapter."

He read, "'For all have sinned, and come short of the glory of God.'"

"These two verses," he said, "tell us that we have all fallen short of what God expects of us and are in need of help in order to restore that relationship with Him.

"The next step is to show that those who are guilty of sin are deserving of the death penalty, but God has given us a way of escape. That's found in Romans 6:23."

He turned and read, "'For the wages of sin is death: but the gift of God is eternal life through Jesus Christ our Lord.'"

"Next we turn to the twelfth verse of the fifth chapter. Pastor, will you please read that for us?"

"Glad to. 'Wherefore, as by one man sin entered into the world, and death by sin; and so death passed upon all men, for that all have sinned.'"

"Again," Nick said, "from this passage we can see that the penalty of sin, which is spiritual death, has fallen upon us all." Then he went on, "The next step along the Romans Road is found in the eighth verse of the fifth chapter of Romans."

Lester raised his hand again.

"Can I read the next one?"

"Of course! Go right ahead."

He read, "'But God comm…comm…'"

"'Commendeth,'" Iris encouraged him.

"'…commendeth his love toward us…in that while we were yet sinners, Christ died for us.'"

"That's great," Nick said. "Iris, how about taking us through the final steps, which are found in the tenth chapter, verses nine through thirteen?"

"Surely." She flipped a couple of pages and read, "'For with the heart, man believeth unto righteousness; and with the mouth, confession is made unto salvation. For the scripture saith, Whosoever believeth on him shall not be ashamed. For there is no difference between the Jew and the Greek: for the same Lord over all is rich unto all that call upon him. For whosoever shall call upon the name of the Lord shall be saved.'"

Nick looked up.

"We can see from this passage, that the only thing anyone has to do to obtain forgiveness of sins, and eternal life, is to accept the free gift of salvation that God has provided. All you have to do is pray: tell Jesus that you accept His offer of salvation and want Him to be Lord and Savior of your life.

"Does anyone have any questions? Lester?"

Lester shook his head.

"Well, let's go through everything one more time:

"Romans 3:10—No one is righteous on their own.

"Romans 3:23—All have sinned, and come short of the glory of God.

"Romans 6:23—The wages of sin is death, but God has provided a way of escape.

"Romans 5:12—Death entered the world through sin.

"Romans 5:8—Jesus Christ, God's son died for our sins.

"And, finally, Romans 10:9-13. Anyone who believes in Christ and confesses Him as Lord and Savior, will be saved."

Lester closed his Bible with a "thump" and stood to his feet.

"I can do this!" he shouted. "Really! I can! I can do this!"

Chapter Eight

LESTER AND IRIS FOR JESUS

Lester was so excited that he wanted to go out "right now" and start knocking on doors.

"I think it's kind of late," Iris said. "We really ought to get an earlier start."

"When, then?" he asked.

"You tell me. You're the one with a job."

"Job? Oh, ya." Lester scratched the back of his head. "Now, let's see. Tomorrow I start work at 7 a.m., which means I'm off at three. Can we go tomorrow afternoon? I can be ready to go by four o'clock."

"I'll come by and pick you up."

"Great. I'll be ready to go!"

Wednesday, December 19th

Lester was true to his word. He was standing out in his driveway waiting for her when she pulled up at 3:45 p.m.

"I knew you'd be early," he smiled, as he climbed in the passenger door of her Pontiac. "You're always early."

"I have to admit, I'm a little nervous," Iris confessed. Lester patted her hand. "There's nothin' to be nervous about," he said. "This is gonna be fun!"

They decided to start out on Fourth Street, where there was a park in the center of a well-kept residential neighborhood. They would leave the car at the park and walk from door to door throughout the neighborhood until their feet gave out.

As Iris carefully maneuvered her huge Pontiac Catalina into a parking space, Lester said, "Now, if you get tired, you let me know, and we can take a break for a while."

Iris smiled, "I'm stronger than I look. But let's take a moment and pray before we get started."

The first house they came to was a small white bungalow surrounded by a picket fence. It was a charming little place, with a flowerbed bursting with color: reds, blues, pinks, purples, yellows, oranges, and every color in-between.

The flowers didn't seem to go with the plastic reindeer on the lawn or the strands of Christmas lights that wound their way around the house, but such is Christmas in California.

The house looked altogether inviting. Lester opened the gate, and Iris walked up on the porch and rang the doorbell. A woman that looked like Mrs. Santa Claus came to the door. She wore her gray hair up in a bun, had ruddy cheeks, and an apron was tied around her waist. The smell of something delicious wafted out through the door, pie? cookies? a cake, perhaps?

"Hello," Iris said. "We're from Friendship Community Church and…"

"I'm sorry, I have not interest", and the woman quickly closed the door.

Next door, a man with a newspaper looked at them through his reading glasses and said, "I'm just not interested. Sorry." Then he politely shut the door.

The third house seemed promising because there was a manger scene set up in the front yard. But nobody answered the door, although Iris and Lester could hear footsteps inside. When Iris put her ear to the door, she thought she heard someone whispering inside. She rang the doorbell again, but no one came.

After ten houses, they hadn't talked to a single soul about Jesus Christ. Nobody was openly hostile, but nobody wanted to listen to what they had to say, either.

"How are you doing?" Lester asked.

"I'm fine," Iris replied. "A little discouraged, though."

Lester shook his head. "Don't you worry," he said. "We're just getting started. My mama always says that you gotta have stick-to-it-iveness." He smiled, "Who knows? Maybe the eleventh time will be the charm."

The next home was a long, brick, ranch-style house with a circular driveway.

"Wow!" Lester exclaimed. "There must be seven bedrooms in there."

"At least," Iris agreed. "Well, here goes."

She rang the doorbell, and a few moments later a thirty-something woman with short, red hair and freckles came to the door. She had a spray bottle in one hand and a dust cloth in the other.

"Hello," Iris said. "We're from Friendship Community Church. If you have a few minutes, we'd like to tell you a little bit about our church and share our faith."

The woman nodded and opened the door. "Come on in," she said, warmly. "I could use a break. That's for sure."

"Cleaning day, huh?" Iris asked.

The woman chuckled. "Every day is cleaning day here. There's always so much to do."

"You have a beautiful house," Iris smiled.

"Thank you," the woman said, as she gestured for them to sit down. "We just moved here from New Jersey a couple of months ago. Oh, by the way, my name is Jane."

"Iris," Iris said, "and this is Lester."

"Pleased to meet you," Lester extended his hand, and Jane took it.

Then, in spite of herself, she began to laugh. "Forgive me for saying so," she chuckled, "but you two don't really seem to go together. You're like, *The Odd Couple* or something."

Iris and Lester looked at each other, and they, too, began to laugh.

Iris was petite, prim, and proper, with every hair neatly in place and two months away from her seventy-fifth birthday.

Lester was 6'3", 235 pounds, shaggy and unkempt. No matter how hard he tried, he couldn't keep his shirttail tucked in.

"Well," Iris chuckled, "we do have something really important in common."

"What's that?" Jane asked.

"We both love Jesus," Iris answered.

It turned out that Jane was lonely. Her husband worked long hours while she stayed home to be a full-time wife and mom to their three school-age kids. In her loneliness she began thinking that there must be something more to life.

By the time they finished sharing their faith, Jane was kneeling in the middle of her living room with tears streaming down her face, surrendering her life to Jesus.

When she finally got up off her knees, her face was radiant.

She grabbed Iris and hugged her tight.

"I'm so glad you came here," she said.

Then she turned to Lester and hugged him.

"Thank you so much!" she said. "I feel like a ten-ton boulder has been lifted from my shoulders!"

As she and Lester headed to the next house down the street, Iris said, "That was absolutely wonderful!"

"Yeah," Lester agreed. "And I just know we're gonna be on a roll now."

Not exactly.

No one in the next three houses was interested.

But at the fourth house, a middle-aged man told Lester and Iris that he had just buried his mother, who had been a strong Christian. He had always been "too busy" for God, but his mother's death had caused him to reassess his priorities. His mother had been so sure that she was going to heaven when she died. He wanted to know how he could have that same assurance.

After listening to Iris and Lester's simple message of faith, He, too, made the decision to receive Christ and said he and his family would be in church on Sunday.

As they left his house, Iris looked at her watch.

"Oh, my goodness! It's nearly seven o'clock."

"Wow!" Lester said, "You mean we've been at this for three hours?"

"I think we ought to call it a day," Iris said.

"I guess so. When do you want to go out again?"

"How about tomorrow?"

"Sure Iris."

On the other side of town, Nick and Pastor Bob had been walking for an hour without success. Dozens of dogs had barked at them. Loud music blared out at them from doors that went unanswered. Half a dozen young mothers came to the door with bawling babies in their arms.

Several people said they were Christians who attended other churches in town. In each case, Pastor Bob wished them well and asked if they had any prayer requests. He and Nick were not interested in taking members away from other churches. Their primary goal was to win souls for Christ, not to increase the membership roster of Friendship Community Church.

And then, they came to a house where a young mother was beside herself because her sick child kept crying, and she didn't know how to calm him down.

When Nick asked if she would like him to pray for the child, she quickly replied, "Oh, yes!" As Nick and Pastor Bob laid hands on the child and prayed, the baby quietly drifted off to sleep in his mother's arms.

"Thank you so much," she whispered. "I'll try to make it to church this Sunday."

Three houses down the street, a forty-something woman came to the door with a shocked look on her face.

The first thing she said when she opened the door was, "Did God send you?"

Nick and Pastor Bob exchanged startled glances, and then Nick said, "Yes, He did. But why…"

She began to cry softly as she opened the door wide and gestured for them to come inside.

Nick and Pastor Bob sat side by side on the couch, while she settled in the easy chair across from them.

"I was just..." she said, and then dissolved into sobs. Nick fished a handkerchief out of his pocket and handed it to her.

She smiled through her tears and dabbed at her eyes.

After a couple of minutes had passed, Pastor Bob encouraged her to continue.

"You were saying?"

She took a deep breath.

"I was...just...praying..." she took another breath, "that God would send someone."

Nick and Pastor Bob both nodded.

"You know, I haven't been to church in at least ten years," she said. "My husband and I used to go every Sunday. But then we got so busy."

She went on to explain that they had crowded God out of their lives. They never even thought about Him anymore.

But two days ago, her husband had told her he had fallen in love with someone else and wanted a divorce. He'd packed up his clothes that night and moved to a nearby motel.

"I haven't done much of anything since then but cry," she told them. "And today, for the first time in years, I was talking to God. Asking Him if He was still there. And if He was, if He still cared about me."

She again wiped at her eyes with Nick's handkerchief.

"I just said, 'God, if you really care, please send someone to let me know.'"

She began to cry again.

Pastor Bob reached out and touched her hand.

"God *is* there," he said. "And he *does* care about you, more than you can imagine."

By the time their day was over, Pastor Bob and Nick were exhausted. They stopped back at the church for a few minutes so the pastor could check his messages.

"This has been a good day," he said, as he sat down behind his desk. "I'm glad you're here. For the first time in a long time, I feel like this church has a fighting chance to survive."

Nick nodded in agreement.

Pastor Bob pressed the button to get his messages.

He had one new message, left at 3:14 p.m.:

"Pastor…this is Jim," said the voice on the machine. Listen, my investors are getting a little restless. I have to have your answer by 9 a.m., one week from today. According to what I hear from my friends at city hall, you don't have much of a choice. Again, if I don't have your agreement to sell by noon, next Wednesday, I'm withdrawing the offer."

CLICK.

Pastor Bob leaned back in his chair as the answering machine stopped.

"What are you going to do?" Nick asked.

"I'm not sure I have a choice. I think we have to accept his offer for the property."

"Maybe not," Nick said. "If we keep knocking on doors…"

Pastor Bob shook his head. "Even if we brought twenty new families into the church—and that's got to be on the high end of optimistic—I'm afraid that it's too late to save this church."

"Why not shoot higher?" Nick smiled. He had developed a genuine fondness for the older man, and wanted to see his ministry succeed.

"I quit shooting for the stars a long time ago," the pastor said, sadly. "One time, when I was a young pastor, I asked one of my older church members why she was always so pessimistic, and you know what she said?"

"No, what?"

"That her pessimism was based on experience." He sighed. "At the time, I felt sorry for her. But, now I know what she was talking about."

Nick kept on smiling. "I may be younger than you, but that doesn't mean I haven't had my share of struggles," he said. "But when I look back, I can see that most of my problems resulted from forgetting the Word of God."

"We need to remember that the Bible says, 'Seek ye *first* the kingdom of God, and his righteousness and all these things will be added unto you.' We're not aiming for personal gain here, Pastor. Our goal is to further the

Kingdom of God, and I just have to believe He's going to bless our efforts."

Pastor McCandlish nodded his head, but it was more to say "I hear you" than "I agree with you." "I hope you're right," he said.

Nick's intention was to fly home on Sunday after the morning worship service. But by Friday evening, he had changed his mind. Exhausted but happy after another long day of knocking on doors, he telephoned Rachel and told her he wanted to stay in Santa Cruz for "a few more days at least. I've got see how this thing turns out."

Rachel wasn't thrilled.

"But Nick! You've already been gone a week!"

"I know. But I just…"

"So I'm going to have to do *all* the Christmas shopping, *all* the decorating, *all* the…"

"I'll make it up to you and the children somehow. But I promise I'll be home for Christmas."

He waited, but there was nothing but silence on the other end.

"Rachel? If it's that important to you, I'll come home tomorrow."

"No," she finally said. "You do what you have to do. We'll be fine."

When he finally hung up the phone, Nick felt unsettled inside. He wanted to rush right home to be with his family.

But, at the same time, he just had to see this thing through.

The first item on Pastor Bob's agenda for Thursday morning was another meeting with Roy Smythe. The purpose of the meeting was to discuss the standing offer to buy the church, but Smythe had something else on his mind.

"Pastor," he said. "I … uh …we … er … that is some of the members. I mean, a couple of … er…"

"What is it, Roy?" the pastor asked. "You're not one to beat around the bush."

"No, I'm not," Roy agreed. "I'm just trying to think of the best way to put this."

"The direct way is usually the best way," Pastor Bob smiled.

"Okay, well…we know that you've been going out from door to door, trying to recruit new members for the church."

"Actually, I've been going out to tell people about Jesus," the pastor corrected him.

"Oh, of course," Smythe waved his hand through the air in a gesture that seemed to mean, *What's the difference?* "Anyway," he went on, "we all appreciate your efforts very much, but the fact is that this Lester fellow isn't…how do I say it? our cup of tea."

The pastor felt his face redden.

Smythe went on.

"We just feel that if he's typical of the new people you're going to be bringing into the church…"

"Roy," Pastor Bob cut in. "First of all, Lester needed to know Jesus. I know he isn't the type of guy you'd want to take to dinner at the country club," he said. "But he has a good heart and he loves God."

"But don't you think he might be more comfortable somewhere else?"

"Roy," the pastor said. "Over the past few days, I think I've rediscovered why this church is here. I had lost sight of the fact that our primary purpose is to be telling people about Jesus."

"But we're doing that, Pastor," Smythe protested. "We've sent missionaries to thirty-three different countries."

"And what are we doing here, at home?" the pastor asked.

Smythe thought hard. "Well, we have that food pantry for the poor."

"I'm all for that," said Pastor Bob. "But the plain truth is that we've grown complacent about our own community. I think that part of our downfall was that the church became missions-centered vs. witness-centered"

Smythe didn't answer.

"I have a feeling Roy," Pastor Bob continued. "I think we can save this church. I'm going to ask the board to request a month's extension on Jim's offer to buy the church."

"You are?" Roy raised his eyebrows.

"Yes," Pastor Bob replied. "And I want you to do me the same courtesy."

"Meaning?"

"Give me a month, and then we'll reevaluate where we stand."

"But Jim said he'll withdraw the offer if we don't sign by Wednesday," Roy sputtered. "We're taking a big chance."

"I know. But I just have a feeling…"

RRRRING! RRRRING!

Pastor Bob thought about letting the answering machine get the phone, but something told him this call might be important.

"Friendship Community Church," he said.

"Pastor Bob?"

"Yes?"

"This is Lester. I'm sorry to bother you. I tried to call Nick first, but he wasn't at Iris's house. And I don't want to worry my mother. She has heart trouble, ya know."

"That's all right, Lester. What can I do for you?"

"Well, the truth is…I've been arrested. Do you think you could come down here to the jail and bail me out?"

"Arrested?" the Pastor exclaimed. "For what?"

"I don't know? I was just…"

"It's okay. Lester," the pastor assured him. "I'll be right there."

Smythe, who had been leaning close, trying to hear as much of the conversation as possible, shook his head and hissed with disgust.

"I knew something like this was going to happen," he said. "I just knew it."

He stood and glared angrily at Pastor Bob.

"Reverend McCandlish," he fumed, "this door-knocking campaign has gone too far! As far as I'm concerned, this Romano fellow is just a pied piper who's leading the entire church astray. I mean, we don't even know this guy!"

Pastor Bob sighed. "We'll have to talk about this later. I've got to get down to the police station."

Chapter Nine

COULD THIS
BE REVIVAL?

Pastor Bob broke into a nervous sweat as he marched up the steps to the Santa Cruz Police Department.

Inside, he waited at the window for several minutes before the clerk finally came to help him.

"I'm here to post bail for Lester Jackson," he said. "What do I need to do?"

"Just a minute, honey, let me see."

Peering down her nose through her reading glasses, she typed something on her computer keyboard and frowned. "This thing is so slow today! Ah…there he is. Are you a family member?"

"I'm his pastor," he said, feeling slightly embarrassed to admit it.

"Do you have some I.D.?"

He pulled out his wallet and removed his driver's license.

"Okay, that's all I need." She handed the license back to him.

"Thank you."

"No problem, sir. He's in the holding cell. I'll have someone take you there. Give me just a minute."

She disappeared into the back. A minute went by, and she didn't return. Two minutes. Three minutes. A whole bunch of minutes.

"Pastor Bob?"

He jumped when someone said his name and tapped him on the shoulder. He hadn't heard anyone come in.

"Oh...hi, Nick."

"Sorry. Didn't mean to startle you. I came as soon as I heard." He looked very worried. "I ran all the way over here."

"How'd you hear about it?"

"I called your office to see if you wanted to have lunch today," Nick explained. "But, one of your elders answered the phone, Roy something or other."

"Smythe."

"Right ... Smythe. He told me that Lester's been arrested."

Pastor Bob nodded. "That's true."

"What for?" Nick asked. "What did he do?"

"I don't know," the pastor sighed. "And apparently he doesn't know either."

Finally, after what seemed like half an hour, the clerk returned to her window.

"I'll be with you in just a moment, sir," she said to Nick.

Nick pointed at Pastor Bob. "I'm with him."

"Oh, well, I'm sorry that I kept you waiting for so long," she said, "but I have some good news for you. The charges have been dropped."

"Dropped?" said Pastor Bob. "Well, that's good. But I still don't understand why he was arrested in the first place?"

The clerk sighed. "As far as I can tell, he didn't do anything. He was picked up on suspicion."

"Suspicion of what?" Nick asked.

"A woman called and said a prowler was peeking in her window. We sent a patrol car to check it out, and they picked him up," the officer explained.

"What did he say?" Nick asked.

"He said he was just going from house to house, knocking on doors, because he wanted to tell people about Jesus. We've had a couple of burglaries over in that part of town recently, so he was brought in for questioning."

"Burglaries?" Pastor Bob shook his head. "I know Lester isn't involved in anything like that."

"Believe me. He's not a suspect," she replied. "Especially not now."

"Especially not now?" the pastor repeated. "What are you talking about?"

"Come on. I'll show you."

She pushed a button to unlock the door that led back to the jail cells. Nick and Pastor Bob followed her down a narrow, dimly lit corridor.

Abruptly, she stopped and stood still, so suddenly that the men almost bumped into her.

She turned to them and put her finger across her lips in a "shushing" motion. "They're still at it," she whispered.

Then she stepped aside to let the men go past her.

They practically tiptoed around the corner into the holding cell area.

There, in front of them, Lester was sharing his faith with the other cellmates. While they sat listening quietly as Lester led them down the Romans Road to salvation.

Later, as they all rode home in Pastor Bob's car, Lester was bubbling over with excitement.

"That was so great!" he exclaimed. "I hope I didn't cause you too much trouble."

"Of course not," his two companions said in unison.

"But why were you going from door to door by yourself?" Nick asked.

"I'm sorry," Lester apologized. "I know you told us to go out in pairs. But I had a couple of hours before I had to be at work, and, to tell you the truth, I've been having so much fun that I just couldn't wait!"

Sunday, December 23rd

Sunday morning, Nick was dressed and ready to leave for church a good fifteen minutes before Iris was ready.

"If you're in such a hurry, maybe you'd better drive," she teased, holding out her keys.

"Glad to," he smiled as he snatched them out of her hand. "Ready?"

"Just keep it under ninety," she laughed.

"I won't go faster than eighty-five," he said. "I promise."

As he drove along, Nick imagined the church parking lot full of cars.

Nick's heart was pounding as they rounded the corner and the parking lot came into view. There it was, just ahead of them.

Dead empty.

Chapter Ten

LET EARTH RECEIVE HER KING

Sunday December 23rd

"Looks like we're the first ones here," Iris said.

Nick looked at his watch. They weren't *that* early.

He felt a knot developing in his throat. He needed to swallow, but his mouth was so dry he couldn't.

"Lord," he prayed silently. "We've worked so hard. We need this victory." He could feel his confidence beginning to weaken.

"Well?" Iris asked.

"Well, what?" Nick croaked.

She extended her hand. "Do you want to go inside, or would you rather sit out here for a while?"

"Oh, sorry." He pulled the keys out of the ignition and handed them to her.

She reached over and gently patted his arm. "I know what you're thinking," she said soothingly, "but don't worry. They'll be here."

Wait a minute! Was that the sound of a car?

Yes! A black Toyota Camry pulled slowly into the church parking lot.

Then it backed out, and headed back down the street in the direction from which it had come.

Oh, Nick sighed to himself. *It was just turning around.*

Nick got out of the car and followed Iris to the church's front door.

Suddenly he felt a bit ashamed. The words of Jesus echoed in his mind, "*O ye of little faith.*"

It didn't really matter if the church was full this Sunday morning. What *did* matter was that the Good News of eternal life through Jesus Christ was being shared, and men, women, and children were coming into God's Kingdom. Once again, he'd lost sight of the power of God's purpose.

"*Seek ye first the Kingdom of God*", he reminded himself.

As he was still mulling things over in his mind, a 1950's vintage red pickup pulled into the lot.

"Oh, look!" Iris exclaimed. "It's the Petersens, and they brought someone with them."

"Who are the Petersens?" Nick asked.

"Some people Lester and I met on Friday," Iris answered. Then she whispered, "They were having a terrible argument when we first got there. It was awful. At first, we were really sorry that we'd knocked on their door. But they turned out to be very nice people."

The passenger-side door swung open, and Lester came sprawling out. "Hey Nick! Hey Iris!"

"Lester!" Nick called. "You're riding in style this morning."

"My house is on their way," Lester explained, as he climbed out of the truck. "Nick, I want you to meet my new friends. This is Bill and Sue."

"Pleased to meet you," Nick said, shaking Bill's hand.

"We're delighted to be here," Bill said.

Bill Petersen looked to be about forty. He was tall and thin, with long hair and a bushy mustache. He wore blue jeans and cowboy boots. Sue wore a simple, flower-print dress and had an open, friendly face.

Nick wasn't really sure how well they'd fit in with the other "better-dressed" members of Friendship Community Church. But he was thankful that, at least, this week's church attendance would be up by two.

"Hey, the Ortegas are here!" Lester said.

Nick turned around and watched as a blue Nissan Altima headed into the lot. Maybe this was going to be a pretty good Sunday after all.

As it turned out, twenty-two new faces were there; however seventy-two people spaced throughout that huge sanctuary didn't seem like very many.

As Nick looked around, he could see that some of the long-time members of Friendship Community Church seemed a bit standoffish and uncomfortable. Perhaps they didn't know what to think of these newcomers. Some of them looked as if they felt their church had been taken over by "outsiders." Roy Smythe and his wife, for example, sat with their arms folded, eyes straight ahead.

Lord, Nick prayed silently, *bring these people together. Please, bring these people together.*

From the pulpit, Pastor McCandlish gave an enthusiastic welcome.

"It's exciting to see so many new faces among us today," he said. "Please stay around after the service so we can get to know you, and if..."

Before he could finish his welcome, a young, blond California surfer stood up. He was perhaps seventeen years old, trim and tan, with golden hoop earrings dangling from both ears.

"Can I say something?" he asked.

"Well, I...sure, go ahead," said Pastor Bob.

"My name is Mike. And I just want to tell you that I was thinking crazy thoughts about killing myself. I didn't think there was anybody in this world who cared about me. And then," he nodded in Lester's direction, "this dude knocks on my door, and tells me..." His voice wavered and he gripped the back of the pew in front of him, trying to regain his composure.

"He tells me ..." and his voice choked "... how much God loves me. I just want to say how much it means to me..." His body began to tremble with sobs and he sat down, unable to finish his sentence.

As he did, Lester got up from his pew, walked over to where Mike was sitting, and put his arm around him. Nick was pleased to see an old-time member of the church, go over and sit down on the other side of Mike.

"Well, Mike," Pastor Bob said, "God does love you, and we're happy to have you with us today."

Next a heavy-set woman in a blue pantsuit stood up. Her husband sat beside her, squeezing her hand.

"Our son was killed by a drunk driver six months ago," she cried. "We didn't know the Lord then. I keep thinking, if you had only come sooner," she hesitated and then continued as tears rolled down her cheeks, "maybe our son would have had a chance to hear about Jesus."

And so it went. One by one, the newcomers stood up to share their faith. And as they did, the walls between old and new began to crumble.

It certainly wasn't the typical Sunday morning worship service. There was no sermon. No hymns. No announcements. But it was wonderful.

Finally, Nick Romano stood up in his pew and addressed the congregation.

"Today," he said, "I would like to take all of you out to knock on doors. There are only two more days until we celebrate Christ's birth. When could there possibly be a better time to go out and share the Good News?"

"I know that some of you don't want to do it," he went on, "that you're afraid. But you don't need to be afraid. People are hungry for God's love."

The woman whose son had been killed by a drunk-driver, jumped to her feet.

"Let's all go to my neighborhood," she said. "I know lots of people who need to know the Lord!"

"Then let's go!" someone shouted.

"I'll lead the way," her husband said.

Almost as one, the members of the congregation got up and made their way to the parking lot.

In a matter of minutes, the "holy caravan" was winding its way through the streets of Santa Cruz.

On the corner of Fourth Street and Primrose Avenue, Seth Hunter sat on his living room sofa, reading the Sunday paper. At thirty-eight, he was bored and depressed and tired of being bored and depressed.

He tossed the newspaper on the coffee table in front of him and sighed.

"There's got to be more to life than this," he said out loud.

From the kitchen, his wife called out, "Did you say something?"

"No, I was just talking to myself," he said.

Suddenly, something outside caught his attention. What were all those people doing out there? There must be close to a hundred of them. And they were headed up the walk, toward his door.

Lester and Iris were the first to reach the Hunter's front door.

"I hope we don't scare them half to death," Iris said.

"It's gonna be a great day!" Lester said. "A really great day."

He rang the doorbell, and then, instinctively he began to sing: "Joy to the world, The Lord is come, Let earth receive her king!"

Laughing at the spontaneity of the moment, everyone joined in to sing the old Christmas carol. Seth opened the door as the carolers continued to sing. "Who are you people? What are you doing here?"

"We're witness caroling!" Lester shouted.

Chapter Eleven

YOU ARE THE LIGHT OF THE WORLD

Monday, December 24th - Christmas Eve

The congregation sat in silent anticipation.

All was dark except for the light from a single slender white candle sitting on the altar at the front of the sanctuary.

Suddenly, Nick's voice rang out.

"In the beginning was the Word, and the Word was with God, and the Word was God....In him was life; and the life was the light of men. And the light shineth in the darkness."

Nick approached the altar and, using the flame from the single white candle, lit two others, and then placed them back in their holders. The church was still dark, but noticeably brighter, as Nick continued reciting from the book of Luke in the Bible:

"And there were shepherds in the same country abiding in the field, and keeping watch by night over their flock. And an angel of the Lord stood by them, and the glory of the Lord shone round about them; and they were sore afraid. And the angel said unto them, Be not afraid; for behold, I bring you good tidings of great joy which shall be to all the people: for there is born to you this day in the city of David a Savior, which is Christ the Lord. And this is the sign unto you: Ye shall find a babe wrapped in swaddling clothes, and lying in a manger. And suddenly there was with the angel a multitude of the heavenly host praising God, and saying, Glory to God in the highest, and on earth peace, good will toward men."

As Nick's eyes grew more accustomed to the darkness, he could see that there were over a hundred people sitting in the large sanctuary. Here and there, the sound of sniffling could be heard, as joy spilled into tears.

He could feel his own joy welling up in his chest. He wasn't sure he could contain it. He wanted to shout, or cry. Or maybe both at the same time.

The presence of Christ was unmistakable. He was there as surely as if He had been walking up and down those aisles, reaching out to comfort with his nail-scarred hands, telling each person present, "I love you! I love you so much that I died for you!"

There was no doubt but that God's fire was beginning to burn in this church—the flames leaping from heart to heart and soul to soul.

Nick believed…no, he knew…that this small church—this group that had been so weak and ineffective just a few days ago-—was now going to turn their city upside down for Christ.

"It has been a joy to be with you for the past several days," Nick said. "I feel now that I am part of you, and know that I always will be."

He paused to gather his thoughts, and then he went on. "Before I came to Santa Cruz, I had been asking myself the question, 'What is God's purpose for my life?' But now I know that our primary purpose is to share the Gospel of Jesus and lead others into a personal relationship with Jesus as their Savior. As Christians we do have an eternal destiny, and the life we live affects eternity forever. You have showed me the power of purpose for my life, and I thank you!

"Never forget that you are the light of the world," he said. "And as Jesus commanded, 'Let your light so shine that men will see your good works, and glorify your Father in Heaven.'"

Next, Pastor Bob came to the altar. He shared that he had been on the verge of giving up—just counting the days until retirement. But now, he felt as if his ministry was just beginning. He couldn't wait to see what the future was going to bring as this church continued to fulfill the prophecy found in the twenty-second Psalm.

He lit another candle.

"If you believe in Jesus, I invite you to come forward and light a candle as a symbol of what He has done in your life and of the faith that burns in your heart."

Then he sat down.

Lester came first. "I don't know what would have happened to me if Nick didn't come to the Waffle House for dinner. For the first time ever, I know my purpose in life."

After sharing his testimony he lit a candle and then gestured at a woman sitting about midway back in the center section. "I'd like you all to meet my mama."

Nobody moved.

"Come on, Mama!" Lester called out. "Stand up and let 'em see you!"

Slowly, a plump, white-haired woman stood and walked to the front, as the congregation responded with an enthusiastic round of applause.

Iris was the next one to the altar.

"I've been in love with Jesus for over sixty years," she said. "And I want you to know that God is faithful. He will never leave you nor forsake you."

And so it went, as numerous church members, new and old, came forward to give their testimony and to light a candle as an expression of their faith in Christ. Each candle gave off only a small glow. But together, they filled the large church with light.

And then, as the shadows from the candle flames danced on the sanctuary walls, Roy Smythe and his wife, Rosemary, rose from their pews and made their way, hand in hand, to the altar.

Roy began talking in the same assured tone he always used. "Rosemary and I have been attending this church for ten years," he said. "But…" and here, his confident bass voice cracked. "I…" and he began to weep.

Rosemary spoke for both of them. "But we've never made a public confession of faith in Christ," she said. "We want to do that now."

Roy could only nod in agreement. "Jesus, we love you," he choked the words out past the lump in his throat.

Pastor Bob was shocked. And overjoyed. But the best was yet to come.

A solitary figure, sitting on the back pew of the center section, got up and stepped into the aisle. He hesitated for a moment, as if he wasn't sure which way to go. It almost seemed as if he wanted to run out the back door—-but he couldn't. An irresistible force was drawing him to the front of the church.

Pastor Bob froze as the man drew closer. It was Jim, the real estate developer who wanted to buy the church.

There was an audible gasp as he stepped to the altar and other members of the congregation recognized him, too.

"My name is Jim Collins," he said. "I attended this church when I was a boy. In fact, Iris here was my Sunday-school teacher, and led me in a prayer to give my life to Jesus when I was ten years old. But when I got older, I started thinking that church was for losers, and I quit coming. Before my mother died, she told me that she prayed every day that I would come back to Jesus. But I didn't care."

He shook his head, "I've been trying to buy this property because I wanted to build an apartment complex here. I've got a lot of power in this town, and I've used it to get this building condemned. I'm sorry..."

He swallowed hard and went on.

"I came by here tonight because I was upset. I heard that something was going on here, and I was afraid it was going to hurt my plans. But now..."

He turned to Pastor Bob. "Pastor, can you forgive me?"

Pastor Bob walked forward to give him a hug.

"I want you all to forgive me," Jim sobbed. "And I want God to forgive me."

"Oh, Jimmy," Iris said. "We love you, and God loves you. Of course, He forgives you!" She rushed forward to give him a hug and a peck on the cheek.

"I'll do anything I can to save this church," the developer sobbed, as members of the congregation gathered around to welcome him home.

HONK! HONK!

As the celebration continued into the night, Nick quietly slipped into Pastor Bob's study, retrieved his suitcase, and then made his way out the back door of the church.

The Super Shuttle was right on time.

HONK!

The driver honked the horn again before he saw Nick headed for his van. Then the driver jumped out, walked around, and opened the back door.

He smiled when he recognized Nick. "You go home now?"

Nick smiled back. "Hello, Fawad. Yes, I'm going home."

He glanced at his watch. There was a non-stop red-eye flight leaving at 10:40 p.m. Pacific standard time. That meant it was just 1:40 a.m. eastern standard time back home in Orlando. If everything went right, he'd get home just as the sun was rising in the eastern sky on Christmas morning.

After all, he had promised Rachel and the children he'd be home for Christmas.

And he just knew that this was going to be the best Christmas ever.

As Fawad steered the Super Shuttle slowly out of the church parking lot and into the street, Nick leaned forward. "Fawad," he said, "are you aware that God loves you very much and has a special purpose for your life?"

"Me, sir?" the driver responded.

Studying Fawad's reflection in the rear-view mirror, Nick saw surprise register in the man's eyes. But there was something more, too.

"I'd like to hear more about this," he said.

"Well let me tell you a story about my family…" Nick began.

Churches in America

Today there are over 270,000 Christian churches in America. 100,000 of these churches are congregations of less than 70 people. The 100,000 smallest churches in America have a larger sphere of influence than the 100 largest churches in America. If the 100,000 smallest churches in America doubled in size we would experience an American revival that would dwarf any former revival in American history. I believe that the simple message of *The Witness Carol* is all that is needed to complete such a task.

"In God's sight there are no little places"
—Francis Schaeffer

Epilogue

I'd like to tell you what happens next for Pastor Bob and the other members of Friendship Community Church.

I'd like to, but I can't...because I don't know.

But I do know one thing. There is a strong core of believers there who have found their eternal destiny through telling others the Good News of abundant life through Jesus Christ. And, really, that's all that matters.

Dietrich Bonhoeffer, a German theologian who was executed by the Nazis during World War II, wrote that one of the marks of the true disciple of Christ is that he doesn't know for sure where he's going next. All he knows is that he's following Christ. To me, that seems to be the only way to live.

The members of Friendship Community Church know that their lives and destinies—both individually and collectively—are in God's hands, and they rest in that. They realize that whatever God has planned for them is better than anything they could possibly plan for themselves.

How about you? Do you have the assurance that you are living as God wants you to? Have you surrendered your will to Him? Have you entered into your eternal destiny by accepting the free gift of salvation offered by Jesus Christ?

If not, you can do it right now. All it takes is a simple prayer of faith. You can follow this example if you'd like:

Lord Jesus, I acknowledge that I am a sinner, and that the wages of sin is death. I also acknowledge that you paid the debt for my sin when You were crucified on the cross of Calvary. I believe that you died in my place, were buried, and rose again on the third day. I ask you to accept me now, to sanctify me and cleanse me through your blood. Come into my heart, and help me live for you each day. It is in Your Holy Name I pray. Amen.

If you have accepted Christ as your Savior, or if you have any other comments about this book, I'd love to hear from you. You may write me at:

George DeTellis Jr.
2500 Sand Lake Road
Orlando FL 32809

george@newmissions.org

Reader's Guide for *The Witness Carol*

The following questions are recommended for group discussion at your Bible Study Group or Sunday school class. The author is available to speak to your reading group via a conference call. To schedule a free conference call with the author please visit his website at www.thewitnesscarol.com

1. Contrast Nick and Rachel's different cultural backgrounds. What were the shared values that were the basis of their marriage?

2. Discuss Jacob's proverb, "It's a sad day, but a joyous one as well," in relationship to Psalm 116:15: "Precious in the sight of the Lord is the death of his saints."

3. Discuss Proverbs 11:30: The fruit of the righteous is a tree of life, and he who wins souls is wise."

4. In chapter one, Nick ponders Proverbs 22:6 "Raise up a child in the way he should go, and when he is old he will not depart from it." Has it been your experience that families train children to share their faith?

5. After Nick prayed, he discovered the book, *The Power of Purpose*, almost immediately. Discuss a time when God answered your prayers nearly instantaneously.

6. Has there been a book, besides the Bible, that has impacted you as profoundly as *The Power of Purpose* impacted Nick?

7. Iris is described as "one vibrant pulse point in a congregation barely hanging on to life." Do you know someone who matches that description?

8. Have you ever been tempted to agree with Jim's statement, "…I only believe in what works"?

9. Describe Roy Smythe, the head of Friendship Community Church's board of elders, using three adjectives. Contrast them with leadership characteristics listed in Titus 1:6-9.

10. What similarities does Lester's first visit to Friendship Community Church have with the visitors described in James 2:1-5?

11. What character best matches this description, found in 1 Timothy 2:15: "Do your best to present yourself to God as one approved, a workman who does not need to be ashamed and who correctly handles the word of truth"?

12. How does the relationship between Iris and Lester confirm the truth of Ecclesiastes 4:9?

13. Read Psalm 22 from beginning to end. What is the implication of the prophecy of the Messiah and the prophecy of the believer's purpose in the same chapter?

14. When the ladies knocked on Nick's grandmother's door in the projects of South Boston, they could not have known the impact their obedience to sharing the Good News would have—both in the current generation and the generations to come. What was the "knock on the door" that brought the Good News to you?

15. Nick concludes his sermon at Friendship Community Church with two questions. *Is your life a random act or do you have a destiny?* And, *What is God's purpose for your life?* Have you answered these questions in your own life?

16. Discuss Lester's enthusiastic entrance into the Kingdom of God in regards to Luke 15:7.

17. "The Romans Road" is a concise group of Scriptures that unfold the need for a Savior, and reveal Jesus as that Savior. What other Scripture verses tell the Gospel story in a concise manner?

18. Nick references Mark 6 as he begins to train the small group gathered at Friendship Community Church. Read Mark 6:7-13 and discuss the implications.

19. Iris suggests that they pray before she and Lester begin sharing the Good News door-to-door. How important is prayer to the sharing of the Gospel?

20. What is a common theme in the lives of all those who were responsive to hearing the gospel from Iris and Lester or Nick and Pastor Bob?

21. Contrast Pastor Bob's pessimism with Ephesians 3:20.

22. Several testimonies were shared at the Candlelight Service. Discuss the possible results, both negative and positive of sharing your own testimony.

23. Friendship Community Church had a tremendous history in "sending life" to the world via missions, but the church itself was dying. Discuss the difference between a missions-centered church and a witness-centered church.

24. Will knocking on doors work in our society today? Why do some very successful religious organizations use this method to recruit new members?

The Witness Carol Church Play

Characters:

Nick Romano

Rachel Romano

Jacob

Greta

Pastor Bob

Iris

Jim

Lester

Roy

Police Officer

Millie Anderson

Sue

Mike

Scene 1

Setting

Dinner table and everyone is just picking at the food. Rachel and Greta are serving.

Jacob

It's a sad day, but a joyous one as well.

Nick

Are you all right? *(Grabs her hand)*

Rachel

Yes, I'll be fine. How about you? You okay?

Nick

(Kisses the top of Rachel's head) Yes, I'm good.

Jacob

I think it will be tough for all of us for a while, I mean Isaac was always good for lively conversation around the dinner table. I think my Greta and your Rachel are going to miss their grandfather for a while. But we will see him again one day. Like I said, it's a sad day but a joyous one as well.

Nick

Yes, there is no doubt he is with the Lord. That is a comfort. He was a fine man with strong convictions and deep faith.

Jacob

There is truth to what you are saying there, Nick. While most of us seem to have our trials and tribulations that sometimes cause us to waver, Isaac was always steadfast. Never knew him to doubt or to question God. Steady he was always the same.

Nick

How can someone be steadfast all the time? Even King David had struggles and hard times.

Greta

Grandpa Isaac has been like that since a child. In fact, his grandfather Henry Keener was an evangelist. He went all through Virginia on horseback, stopping in every little town and village he came to, just helping out wherever he could. He'd help build fences, shoe horses, and pick apples, whatever he could.

Jacob

And all the time he was helping he was talking to non-believers about Jesus, urging them towards salvation. And if they were believers, he'd be talking to them about serving and discipleship. He was on fire for the Lord. And Isaac was just like his father.

Lights go dim and everyone around Nick acts like they are still talking but the focus is on Nick. Also everyone could freeze while Nick says his next lines.

Nick

Isaac had such a passion for Jesus…where is my passion? Where did it go? Me…Mr. Evangelist I'm the one who is suppose to go around to different churches and get everyone on fire for Jesus! Maybe my mission is over? Maybe I was called to be an evangelist for a time? And that season has passed. All I know is that I am so tired. Maybe I should just let that small fire in my belly burn out? Oh Lord, help me! Show me the way and teach me whatever it is I need to learn to do your will. All I have ever known is to go into the world and preach the gospel and that is all I ever wanted to do…it was my passion, my hearts desire…but now I am so tired. Oh Father I can't seem to do what I need to do anymore. Please re-light the fire inside me. Oh please use me again.

Lights go back up or everyone unfreezes.

Jacob
So we went ahead and sorted through Isaac's belongings and Lord knows he didn't have much but we saved his bible to give to you Rachel. We thought he would want you to have it.

Rachel
Oh thank you Jacob. I will cherish it as long as I live.

Jacob
Now Nick, we wanted to give you something to remember Isaac by and as you know he had many books, theological works, inspirational too. And I know how much you like to read, unlike me, so Greta and I would like you to help yourself to some of Isaac's books. They are over there in the barrel. He wasn't partial to bookshelves.

Nick goes over to the barrel in the corner of room and opens it and pulls out various things. He finally pulls out an old beat up small book. He blows off the dust on the book. He begins to open it and reads the first page.

Nick

This book is a gift to my children…and to my children's children yet to be born. May you discover your power of purpose hidden in God's Word, Psalm 22. Henry Keener, August 12, 1929. *(Looks at cover of book)* The Power Of Purpose, 1907. *(Pause)* This book belonged to your great grandfather, Henry Keener. *(Looks towards heaven)* Are you trying to tell me something?

BLACKOUT

Scene 2

Nick is in his study reading.

Rachel

Honey dinner is ready in five minutes.

Nick

Okay, I will be right there to set the table.

Rachel

Don't worry about it, I have already done it. You know that must be some book! You have been hiding in here since we got home from the funeral.

Nick

I have? Well you are right it is some book!

Rachel

Five minutes don't forget! *(She starts to leave)*

Nick slowly closes the book.

Nick

Wow! I wonder if what's in this book really works? *(Calls out to her and she turns back around.)* Rachel, I got to go out there and see. I'm going to get back out there and preach this as if I really do believe it. *(Rachel hugs him.)*

Rachel

Good for you dear, ooh…dinner I think I may be burning it. *(Continues off stage)*

Nick

And if it doesn't work, than I'm quitting the ministry and going into real estate!

BLACKOUT

Scene 3

Setting
Only a pulpit and a few chairs.

Iris

Pastor Bob thanks for the lesson tonight. Too bad only eleven people showed up.

Pastor Bob

Thanks Iris. I was just thinking about what was on the television tonight? I always seem to be competing with some program.

Iris

Well see you Sunday. *(Iris leaves)*

Pastor Bob goes to the pulpit and collects his bible and slowly walks to a chair and sits down. Jim comes up through the auditorium.

Jim

So did you have a big crowd tonight? What five…six…show up?

Pastor Bob

Eleven!

Jim

Eleven! Wow! How'd you fit them all into this auditorium? What does it hold…five…six…hundred!

Pastor Bob

You can just skip the sarcasm and get down to business.

Jim

I'm only trying to make a point!

Pastor Bob

Which is?

Jim
It's about time for you and that board of yours to stop stalling and accept my offer. You just don't need this big building any more. *(Pause)* The two million dollars that I am offering you is a lot of money. You can buy yourself a nice little place somewhere and start over.

Pastor Bob
Yes, I know, but…

Jim
Oh, by the way, I've got some good news. The city planning commission just approved my plans. I'm going to knock down this old church and bring it into the 21st century. The way of the future…is with garden apartments!

Pastor Bob
Look Jim, we are pretty close to making a decision.

Jim
Decision? What decision do you have to make? I don't want to be cruel, but your church has outlived its usefulness. Nobody is interested in hearing your old fashioned ideas about God!

Pastor Bob
Jim, How can you say that in fact, I know you were raised in this church. I knew your father and he was a fine man of God. Where did you go wrong?

Jim

I'm sorry if I hurt your feelings, Pastor but these days I only believe in what works. And from where I sit, it's obvious that whatever you're doing here…it just isn't working. You've got my offer. I'll need your answer…soon before the first of the year. *(Jim leaves)*

Pastor Bob

Oh Lord, help us.

Phone rings again. Bob is startled and looks at the phone and then up towards heaven.

Pastor Bob

(Answers phone) Hello?

On the other side of the stage spot comes up on Nick.

Nick

Reverend McCandish?

Pastor Bob

Yes?

Nick

This is Nick Romano. I'm calling to follow up the letter I sent you last week, in fact I had sent you four letters and I had not heard back from you so I decided to call.

Pastor Bob

I'm sorry Mr. Romano, we are without a church secretary at the moment and I'm a little bit behind in my correspondence.

Nick

That's okay, I understand that you are a busy man but if you have a moment right now why don't you check your calendar and let me know when would be a good time for me to come and speak.

Pastor Bob

I don't want to be rude, but the truth is there won't be a good time.

Nick

I don't understand, I know your church is…

Pastor Bob

I'm sorry, but frankly we are not doing well financially right now and our attendance is way down. There is no way we could pay your travel expenses or provide an honorarium. Especially not with Christmas just around the corner.

Nick

Listen Pastor, I hear what your saying but…something happened to me recently and for the first time in a long while, I'm really excited about reaching people for Christ. I think I could get the members of your congregation excited, too. If you'd just let me come and preach.

Pastor Bob

There is not many to preach at…in fact, tonight we only had eleven people and that counted me and the praise and worship leader and the piano player.

Nick

That is not going to get me down.

Pastor Bob

All right, you can come next Sunday. But don't expect too much from this congregation. I wouldn't want you to lose your newfound excitement. *(Hangs up phone)*

Bob sits down feeling rejected. Enter Roy with stacks of papers and files.

Roy

Pastor Bob, what's wrong?

Pastor Bob

Everything! And by the look on your face I just bet it's going to get worse!

Roy

You're right, it's not good. *(Sits down)* We need to borrow money again this month to pay our utility bills. And here is a threatening letter from the city. *(Hands him the letter)* Basically it says, that we need to get everything up to code within the next 60 days, or their going to condemn the church.

Pastor Bob
Sixty days! That list is so long there is not way we could get that fix even if we had the money!

Roy
I know, including the roof problems the cost is a little over $900,000! There is no way our congregation can raise that much money! *(Pause)* I saw Jim leaving just now, he was laughing when he told me that the only thing our church needs now is a decent burial.

Pastor Bob
That's what hurts the most, he is probably right.

Roy
Well I told him that we needed time to find another building to rent. Most of our members seem to think the same thing. In fact, they feel that a new location might help us gain some new members.

Pastor Bob
I don't know? Sometimes I think we should sell the church property for $2 million dollars and give the money to the Missions board and close the doors forever. That way, at least we'd know the money was going for something important. Oh that reminds me a missionary called me today and wants to come to our church next Sunday and speak.

Roy
You told him no, right?

Pastor Bob

Well actually he wouldn't take no for an answer. He has this excitement in his voice and told me that he felt that this message is for our church. I told him there wasn't much left here. But he was adamant!

Roy

Well, I wonder how he's going to feel after he comes here?

Pastor Bob

Probably just like we feel…disappointed.

BLACKOUT

Scene 4

Setting
A few tables set like a restaurant.

Nick walks in and looks around. Only one in there is Lester, who is in worn out faded jeans and a lumberjack plaid shirt and a dirty apron and a baseball cap.

Lester

Evenin. Sit anywhere you want.

Nick

Not so busy tonight?

Lester

No sir, we ain't busy a' tall. Why we was busy about seven o'clock, and then another bunch of folks come in around eight, or maybe it was seven forty-five? Anyways it don't matter to me, cause when we ain't busy I got time to think. And I like taking time to think, don't you?

Nick

Well I…

Lester

I used to be night clerk over to the Quality Inn, and I loved that job cause it gave me lots of time to think. Except sometimes it would get real busy, you know what I mean? Hey, you're new around these parts, ain't you? I ain't never seen you a' fore. Well my name is Lester. *(Sticks out hand to shake Nicks)*

Nick

I'm Nick.

Lester

Nick? I used to know a guy named Nick. You wouldn't be related to him, would you?

Nick

Well, I wouldn't know if….

Lester

He was a real nice ol' boy.

Nick

I'm sure he was…uh listen do you think I could order grilled chicken sand…

Lester

Why of course you can! You can order anything you want. A grilled chicken sandwich, a cheeseburger, a ham and cheese on rye, a French dip sandwich. We got them all…anything you want. Hey, you want a waffle? We specialize in waffles. That's why we're called the Waffle House on account of we specialize in waffles…in fact we gots all kinds…Belgian waffles, blueberry waffles, harvest grain waffles…*(Enter Mr. And Mrs. Johnson)* Howdy, Mr. And Mrs. Johnson, how are y'all doing tonight?

Mrs. Johnson

We're fine Lester, how's your mama?

Lester

Oh she's fine. 'Cept you know she worries about me when I have to work late. Oh my, where are my manners? This is my new friend Nick.

Everyone smiles at one another.

Lester

Now what was that you wanted? A grilled chicken sandwich?

Nick

Yes that's right.

Lester
No prob…be back in a jiffy.

Lester walks over to the Johnson's.

Mr. Johnson
I'm surprised you're still working here, Lester. I thought you were going to take that job over at the car dealership?

Lester
Nah didn't work out.

Mrs. Johnson
What about your plans to go back to school?

Lester
Didn't work out neither, but that's okay if I wasn't working here I wouldn't a met no nice people like y' all. Hey Mr. Nick, ya didn't never tell me why you are here in town. Visiting relatives?

Nick
As a matter of fact, I'm preaching tomorrow at Friendly Community Church. The service starts at 10. I'd love to see you there, Lester.

Lester
I'll have to check my schedule. I think I'm working in the morning.

Nick

Well I hope you can make it. Thanks for the good sandwich and the conversation. Good night.

BLACKOUT

Scene 5

Setting: Pulpit and two chairs facing the congregation

Pastor Bob

Good morning and welcome. Today we are fortunate to have a guest speaker who…

Lester comes in the back doors of your sanctuary. He stops and looks around. He spots Nick and as he comes down the isle he waves at Nick. Nick waves back and smiles.

Pastor Bob

Who has come a long way. His name is Nick Romano.

Nick stands up and goes to pulpit and shakes the Pastor's hand and then turns towards the congregation.

Nick

Thank you Pastor. I want to ask you a question today. Is there a purpose for your life? Let me ask you again, does your life have meaning? Or is it just a series of random experiences? Are you moving toward a goal or are you like a feather floating around in the breeze? Before we consider that question too deeply, I want to tell you a little about who I am and why I am here. I am a product of three women who came and witnessed to my grandmother years ago. My father was saved early in his life and became a preacher of a great church in Massachusetts, but when I was 18 years old my dad felt God calling him to Haiti to preach the gospel. Haiti? Where was that? I had to look it up and I was shocked! Haiti is the poorest nation in the western hemisphere. A place where people are hungry where they don't have things like running water electricity or plumbing. Haiti is a land of Voodoo and repression and I didn't want to go there!

But apparently it is what God wanted…my family has been living and working there for 20 years now. The Lord has used us to build schools, to feed the hungry and most importantly of all to bring thousands of hearts out of the darkness and into the light of God's love. I know, and my family knows that none of this would have happened without those three women. Because of those women who had the courage to knock on someone's door nearly fifty years ago…thousands of people have come to accept Christ as Savior and will live with Him forever.

(Nick knocks on the pulpit three times) Their simple knock on that door is still echoing into all eternity! I don't know those women's names but when I get to heaven I will meet them face to face and I'll enjoy telling them that I'm part of their inheritance. That I wouldn't be there if it wasn't for their faith and courage.

Lester sneezes really loud and Nick stops and looks at him.

Nick

Bless you brother…now where was I? Let's get back to the question I asked you. Is your life a random act or do you have a destiny? And if you do have a destiny, what is God's purpose for your life? The answer is that God has a plan for each and every one of us.

He says so in the book of Jeremiah: For I know the plans I have for you, plans to prosper you and not to harm you, plans to give you hope and a future. But the fact is if you have never surrendered your life to Jesus your life is nothing more than a feather bouncing around in the winds of chance.

A few months ago I had reached the point where I was just lurching along through life, doing the best I could, and hoping that God would bless me. Then I made a discovery that changed everything. *(Holds up the old book)* This book is over 90 years old and it contains wisdom that our generation has largely forgotten.

I want you to notice in 22nd Psalm verse 30: A seed shall serve him: it shall be accounted to the Lord for a generation. They shall come and declare his righteousness unto all people that shall be born that he hath done this.

We who belong to Christ are that seed, our destiny is to declare what God has done! We are to declare the good news of Jesus Christ!

The knock at the door of my grandmother's house is still echoing today. It don't know who those women were, I don't know their names. But they single handedly changed the course of one family forever.

This book helped me understand that far too many of us are missing out on what God wants us to accomplish. So many people feel inadequate, I don't have a bible degree...I'm not ordained...I'm too old...I'm too young...I'm too poor...I'm too busy...Our consciousness of our own unworthiness cripples us from reaching out and telling somebody about Jesus. Whoever you are...a student...a businessman...a cook...you have a sphere of influence that God has given only you. No one can impact the people in that sphere the way you can.

We are doing everything we can to tell people in foreign lands about the salvation that comes only through faith in Christ... and that is good...but what are we doing right here in our own neighborhoods?

We feed third world countries but the people we come in contact with everyday...our friends and neighbors are starving! I have brought enough copies of this book for all of you. I hope you'll all read it. If you put it into practice, I know it will revolutionize your life and it will bring new life to this church. This morning I'm knocking at your door and I'm giving you an invitation to give your life to Jesus...will you?

Lester stands up

Lester
Yes! Yes! I'll give my life to Jesus now! *(He runs down front and starts to cry and Nick embrace him and they say the sinner's*

prayer.) This is the happiest day of my life? I'm so glad you wanted that grilled chicken sandwich.

BLACKOUT

Scene 6

Setting: Restaurant

Iris

I can't even begin to tell you how thrilled I was to hear what you had to say this morning. You know our church hasn't been doing very well over the last few years and…

Pastor Bob

No it sure hasn't. *(Pause)* I believe God brought you here for a purpose.

Iris

So do I!

Pastor Bob

But do you really think this will work…in this day and age?

Nick

Well, to tell you the truth, Pastor McCandlish, I've never done this before. I just found this old book a few weeks ago, and it was so exciting. It made me think that if I…

Pastor Bob

You were right you had to come to our church this morning. But now you have to deliver the results.

Nick

Deliver the results? What do you mean?

Pastor Bob

Look we need help, I want you to stay around just for a week or so and help us put your message into practice.

Nick pulls out his calendar and checks to see if he can stay. He is really stalling for time.

Iris

You can stay in my guest room and I'll fix all your meals. I'm a very good cook rev…er…Nick. What do you say?

Nick

Well, I'm tempted by the cooking offer. *(Laughs)* I will have to call my wife.

Iris

Yeah, when can we start?

BLACKOUT

Scene 7

Setting: Church, maybe a couple of chairs in a circle. Nick and Pastor Bob are talking to Iris. Enter Lester.

Lester

Good evening all. My boss gave me the evenin' off. I read the book, I'm not a good reader but I read every word. Now I'm ready to get out there and start telling people about Jesus.

Nick

I have a feeling that the Lord is really going to use you Lester.

Lester

Imaging God using me?

Iris

Lester, I have a present for you, *(she hands him a bible).*

Lester

A bible? I've never had a bible before, thanks Miss Iris.

Pastor Bob

Well it is 7:15 and it looks like this is all that is coming. So we might as well get started. So Nick why don't you start things off.

Nick

We have to trust God has brought the people He wants to be here tonight. And remember He used only 12 apostles to turn the entire world upside down, He can certainly use the 4 of us to transform this town. Let me tell you about two women who came knocking at my grandmother's door one Saturday afternoon, not too long after my grandfather was killed.

They were Christians who told my grandmother about Jesus. On that day in the kingdom of God came into the Romano family. Those women invited my family to come to church. That's what she did; she took all eight of her children to church and gave her heart to Jesus. Every Sunday after that, she was in that church, with all of her children sitting besides her.

My grandmother was never the same after that day. She had joy and excitement every day of her life because Jesus Christ came into her life and filled it with His love. The bible says to send forth two by two…and again Jesus commissioned us to go out into all the world and preach the gospel to everyone. He sent them out in pairs also. I think that this is very important.

Iris
(Looks at Lester) We are going to make a great team!

Nick
The book I gave you talks about going door-to-door witnessing. We don't go alone…we bring the Holy Spirit with us. There is no limit as to what God can do; all He asks is that we have an open heart and a willingness to let Him work through us.

Remember you are bringing the good news to the lost. Some people may laugh at you or make fun of you. They may just turn their backs on you and leave you standing there. But most people will listen if they know you're sincere and as they listen to you they'll hear God's Holy Spirit talking to them, and the truth will take hold in their hearts.

I know that there are only four of us but we can go out there and turn this town upside down for Jesus.

Lester

Preacher, I don't mind going and knocking on doors but what do I say if someone invites us in? I mean, this is all new to me and I sure don't want to mess things up. My mama always said to me, "Lester, the best way to make people think you're smart is to keep your mouth shut!" In other words if you don't know anything about something, but go ahead and pretend like you do, people are going to see right through that and they'll…

Nick

I understand, that is why I have here, this…*(Hands them each a piece of paper)* this is the Romans Road and it is a very effective method of evangelism. This method of leading people to salvation is based entirely on Romans. It all begins with the tenth verse of the third chapter. I suggest that you mark that verse in your bible and then mark the next verse you'll need and so on…

Lights go dim. Everyone changes positions…Lester is off stage with Iris.

Pastor Bob

Nick, that was the most rewarding thing I have ever done. And I am a preacher for 20 years and have seen and done a lot. But tonight when we were witnessing door to door…it was…well I have to admit at first I was scared. What will people think? Will they know my church is failing? Will they want to listen to me? But when I took me out of the picture and let the Holy Spirit take over....BAM!!! Things start happening!

Nick

I know I was also a bit reluctant to see if this book really works. Especially when we went to about 6 houses that wouldn't even let us through the door. I was about to give up and go home and sell real estate. But I am glad that we did not give up. When that woman opened the door and asked us if God had sent us, I wanted to shout...YES!!!

Pastor Bob

She was crying so much it was hard to understand her, but she said she was praying that someone would come to help her. I don't understand how people get so busy that they cut God out of their lives.

Nick

It happens...and it happens way too much. But it sometimes takes a tragedy to get peoples attention.

Enter Iris and Lester and they stop to listen.

Pastor Bob

And I would say that young woman was devastated that her husband was leaving her for another woman. But she had been praying and said to God if you are real then send someone... and then we knocked on the woman's door.

Lester

God is real and He cares for all of us.

Iris

Yes He does. I don't know how it went with you. But we had a lot of rejection. In fact one woman slammed the door in Lester's face.

Lester

I counted, it took us 10 houses till someone let us come in and tell them about Jesus. TEN!!! TEN!!!

Iris

Lester is right. It was a huge house and she had a ton of kids. Actually I think she just wanted a break from her everyday routine. And I think she wanted to talk to someone above the age of 9.

Nick

That's okay, doesn't matter why someone let's you in, any opportunity is a good opportunity to talk about Jesus. So how did it go?

Lester

She laughed at us.

Pastor Bob/Nick

What?

Lester

That's right she laughed at us...said we don't look like we belong together. Said we was like the Odd couple?

Iris

What she said couldn't have been more perfect...I told her that we may look different but we have something in common. We both love Jesus. We go to find out that Jane, that's her name, is lonely. Her husband works long hours and her day is full of just kids and she had been wondering if this was all life was about.

Lester

Fifteen minutes later she and I were kneeling in front of her couch and I led her to the Lord. Me...Lester...I can't believe this.

Iris

We then invited her and her family to come to church this Sunday and let's see how many more did we invited...Lester?

Lester

(*Proudly*) Four other families. Hey preacher, can we do this again?

BLACKOUT

Scene 8

Setting: Church

Jim

Pastor, I am afraid that this is the end of the road. My investors are getting a little restless and I have to have your answer by 12 noon one week from today. And according to what I hear from friends at city hall, you don't have much of a choice. Again if I don't have your agreement to sell by noon next Wednesday, I'm withdrawing the offer. Do I make myself perfectly clear?

Pastor Bob
Yes I understand. I will have an answer for you by then.

Jim
I will be waiting to hear from you, good-bye.

Nick
He seems like a real sour puss!

Pastor Bob
He is always trying to spoil the fun.

Nick
What are you going to do?

Pastor Bob
I'm not sure I have a choice. I think we have to accept his offer for the property.

Nick
Maybe not! If we keep knocking on doors...

Pastor Bob
Even if we brought twenty new families into the church...
and that is on the high end of being optimistic, it wouldn't be enough to make a dent in what we owe.

Nick
Why not shoot higher?

Pastor Bob
I quit shooting for the stars along time ago.

Nick
I too was starting to think like that...but the bible says seek ye first the kingdom of God and all these things will be added unto you. We are not asking for personal gain here.

Our goal is to further the kingdom of God. And I just have to believe that He is going to bless our efforts.

Pastor Bob
I hear you...and I hope you are right.

Roy and a few male members enter.

Roy
Pastor Bob, you are just the person we want to see.

Nick
Looks like a lynching posse. I'll see you tonight at 7. Remember seek His kingdom first.

Pastor Bob
I'll remember. Okay Roy what's up? Why are all the board members here? I don't remember calling an elders meeting today.

Roy

You didn't. It seems that we have noticed…that…well…it looks…like…

Pastor Bob

Get to the point Roy!

Roy

Okay! We understand that you have been going door to door trying to recruit new members for the church.

Pastor Bob

Well actually, I've been going out to tell people about Jesus.

Roy

Oh of course! What's the difference?

Pastor Bob shakes his head.

Roy

Anyway, we all appreciate your efforts very much, but the fact is that this Lester fellow isn't…how do we say…our cup of tea!

Pastor Bob

What?

Roy

We just feel that if he's typical of the new people you're going to be bringing into this church…then…

Pastor Bob

Roy! First of all, Lester needed to know Jesus. The bible says that the angels in heaven rejoice over every sinner who comes to repentance and I would hope that we would join them. I know that Lester isn't the type of guy you want to take to a fancy dinner at your country club Roy, but he has a good heart and he loves God. Besides haven't you ever heard it said that a church is supposed to be a hospital for sinners and not a museum for saints?

Roy

Is that supposed to be funny? Cause it's not! In fact, I have never heard that saying before in my life! Don't you think that Lester would be more comfortable some place else?

Pastor Bob

Roy, over the past few days, I think I've rediscovered why this church is here. I had lost sight of the fact that our number one job has to be telling the lost about Jesus.

Roy

I think that is what we have been doing…we've sent missionaries to 33 different countries.

Pastor Bob

But what have we been doing here? In our own town?

Roy

We have a food pantry.

Pastor Bob

Not enough! We have to feed their souls not just their stomachs. I have a feeling Roy that we can save this church. In fact, as long as we have all the board members here I want to request that we take a month extension on that offer.

Roy

A month? But the offer expires next Tuesday at noon!

BLACKOUT

Scene 9

Setting: Jail cell. Pastor Bob is there paying bail for Lester. Enter Nick.

Nick

Bob, what's happened?

Pastor Bob

How did you get here?

Nick

I called the church and one of your elders answered and said you were here bailing out Lester? Is that true?

Pastor Bob

True. Don't know what he did yet.

Out walks Lester smiling.

Nick
Lester! Are you okay?

Lester
Yea preacher I am.

Nick
Why were you brought in here?

Lester
Well…

Police person
It seems that Lester here was picked up on suspicion of looking in windows. Apparently he was going door to door telling everyone about Jesus and someone got spooked and called us. We have had several burglaries in that part of town so we brought him in for questioning.

Nick
Burglaries! I know that Lester is not involved in that.

Police person
Believe me he is not a suspect. Especially not now!

Pastor Bob/Nick
What?

Police Person
Lester has been telling all of us all about Jesus. How He changed his life and how He can change our lives. You just missed us all kneeling down by that desk over there praying.

Lester
Led them down the Romans road to salvation, preacher, just like you taught me to.

Nick
Well I'll be…*(everyone freezes)* God you are awesome. Your word is true. I guess I won't be selling real estate any time soon.

BLACKOUT

Scene 10

Setting: Church. Pastor Bob, Nick, Iris and Lester are watching everyone come into the church.

Iris
There are the Peterson's and look they brought a friend.

Lester
And there is Mrs. Stone and all her children…yep they are all there…I just counted them. And look Miss Iris…that's her husband. She thought he wouldn't have time for going to church. Remember?

Iris
Yes Lester, I remember. I can't believe this. All week we went door-to-door witnessing and led many to the Lord. But I wasn't sure they would all show up here at our church.

Pastor Bob
Iris I was thinking the same thing. Oh us of little faith!

They all laugh.

Lester
Hey look it's the guys from the police station…and they brought their families. God is so good.

Nick
Yes Lester God is so good to us.

Pastor Bob
Thank you all for coming and let me say that I am very pleased to see so many new faces. I hope you all will come again. I would love for all of you to stay and get to know each other. I know that our old members would like to greet everyone who is new today. Let's take a few minutes to get to know each other.

Everyone gets up and starts to talk to each other. Roy and his wife just sit there.

Mike
Hi my name is Mike and I want to thank you for knocking on my door. I was just thinking about taking my life, because I

felt that no one cared about me. Then you showed up and told me about Jesus and how He loves me. Thank you, Lester.

Sue

Our marriage was in trouble and we were fighting all the time. We now see that we have both been selfish since we surrender our lives to Jesus. Thank you Iris for knocking on our door.

Millie

My name is Millie Anderson and Nick and Reverend Bob knocked on our door. I didn't even want to answer it, but they were persistent. I let them into my house and listened to what they had to say. I told them that I was a single parent and that my life had no meaning. I felt so convicted that I gave my heart to Jesus that day. But what I didn't tell them was that a drunk driver killed my son six months ago. We didn't know the Lord then, in fact we figured we had lots of time left to get around to God. If only you had come sooner…maybe my son would have had a chance to hear about Jesus.

BLACKOUT

Scene 11

Setting: Church

SONG: JOY TO THE WORLD

Pastor Bob

(Lights one candle) And there were shepherds in the same country abiding in the field and keeping watch by night over

their flocks. And an angel of the Lord stood by them and the glory of the Lord shone round about them and they were afraid. And the angels said unto them be not afraid for behold I bring you good tidings of great joy which shall be to all the people for there is born to you this day in the city of David a savior which is Christ the lord and this is the sign unto you: you shall find a babe wrapped in swaddling clothes and lying in a manger. And suddenly there was with the angel a multitude of the heavenly host praising God saying glory to god in the highest and on earth peace among men in whom he is well pleased.

Nick

(Lights one candle) It has been a joy to be with you for the past several days. I feel now that I am part of you and know that I always will. These last few days have been among the best of my life and the flame of faith and hope has been rekindled in me as I have seen the power of God's love working through you. Never forget that you are the light of the world and Jesus commanded Let your light so shine that men will see your good works and glorify your Father in heaven.

Lester

(Stands up and lights one candle) I don't know what would have happened to me if Nick hadn't decided to come to the Waffle house for dinner. For the first time ever, I feel as if I have a purpose in my life.

Iris

(*Stands up and lights a candle*) I've been in love with Jesus for over 60 years and I want you to know that He'll never let you down.

Many other members start to come down and light candles. Music is playing. Choir is singing. As the last member gets up to light a candle Jim stands up and goes forward. Pastor Bob sees him and goes towards him.

Jim

My name is Jim Jones and I attended this church when I was a boy. In fact, Iris here was my Sunday school teacher and led me in a prayer to accept Jesus. But when I got older I started thinking that church was for losers and I quit coming. Before my mother died she told me that she prayed every day that I would come back to Jesus. But I didn't care. I've been trying to buy this property because I wanted to build an apartment complex here. I've got a lot of power in this town and I've used it to get this building condemned. And I'm sorry...I came by here tonight because I was upset. I heard that something was going on here and I was afraid it was going to hurt my plans. But now...Pastor can you forgive me? I want you all to forgive me...and I want God to forgive me.

All hug Jim.

Jim

I'll do anything I can to save this church.

Lester
God is so good.

Pastor Bob
Yes Lester, God is so good.

BLACKOUT